Chinese Myths and Legends

Ancient myths and legends can be seen to represent a repository of the wisdom and imagination of our ancestors. *Chinese Myths and Legends* introduces the stories of deities, heroes and the origins of the universe that underpin the spirit of traditional Chinese culture. Utilizing a variety of ancient Chinese sources, Chen Lianshan examines the origin and development of myths and legends in China, including both well-known and less familiar traditions, and compares these traditions to the mythology of the ancient Western world.

Introductions to Chinese Culture

The thirty volumes in the Introductions to Chinese Culture series provide accessible overviews of particular aspects of Chinese culture written by a noted expert in the field concerned. The topics covered range from architecture to archaeology, from mythology and music to martial arts. Each volume is lavishly illustrated in full color and will appeal to students requiring an introductory survey of the subject, as well as to more general readers.

Chen Lianshan

CHINESE
MYTHS & LEGENDS

CAMBRIDGE
UNIVERSITY PRESS

CAMBRIDGE UNIVERSITY PRESS
Cambridge, New York, Melbourne, Madrid, Cape Town,
Singapore, São Paulo, Delhi, Tokyo, Mexico City

Cambridge University Press
The Edinburgh Building, Cambridge CB2 8RU, UK

Published in the United States of America by Cambridge University Press,
New York

www.cambridge.org
Information on this title: www.cambridge.org/9780521186797

Originally published by China Intercontinental Press as
Chinese Myths and Legends (9787508513232) in 2009

© China Intercontinental Press 2009

This updated edition is published by Cambridge University Press
with the permission of China Intercontinental Press under
the China Book International programme ☙.

For more information on the China Book International programme, please visit
http://www.cbi.gov.cn/wisework/content/10005.html

Cambridge University Press retains copyright in its own contributions
to this updated edition

© Cambridge University Press 2011

First published 2011

Printed and bound in China by C&C Offset Printing Co., Ltd

A catalogue record for this publication is available from the British Library

ISBN 978-0-521-18679-7 Paperback

Contents

Preface   1

The Origin of the Universe   5

    I. Chaos   6

    II. The Beginning of the World   6

The Origin of Humankind   9

    I. The Image of Nüwa   10

    II. The Creator of Human Beings   10

    III. Nüwa Mending the Heaven   11

    IV. Nüwa and Marriage   14

    V. The End of Nüwa   16

Universe in Myth   17

    I. The Heaven and Earth   18

    II. Ten Suns and Twelve Moons   20

    III. Mount Kunlun: City of Deities on Earth   22

    IV. Deities' World in the Sea   26

    V. Capital of Ghosts and Taodu Mountain   28

Fuxi, the God of East Heaven   31

I. The Birth of Fuxi   32

II. Fuxi and Nüwa: Human Creator and Goddess of
Marriage   33

III. Cultural Civilization of Fuxi   37

IV. Fuxi, the God of East Heaven   41

Yandi, the God of South Heaven   43

I. The Contribution of Emperor Yandi   44

II. Later Generations of Emperor Yandi   47

III. Chaos in Emperor Yandi's Era   50

Emperor Huangdi, the God of Central Heaven   51

I. The Birth of Emperor Huangdi   52

II. The War between Emperor Huangdi and
Emperor Yandi   52

III. War between Emperor Huangdi and Chiyou   53

IV. Xingtian Scrambles for the Throne   60

V. The Daily Life of the Central God Huangdi   62

VI. The Contributions of Emperor Huangdi and his
Subordinates   64

Shaohao, the God of West Heaven and Zhuanxu,
the God of North Heaven   71

I. Shaohao in Chinese Myth   72

II. Birth of Zhuanxu   76

III. Cutting off the Link between Heaven and Earth   78

IV. War Between Zhuanxu and Gonggong   79

 V. The Origin of the Mengshuangshi Tribe   81

VI. The End of Zhuanxu   81

VII. The Offspring of Zhuanxu   83

Myths in the Era of Emperor Diku   85

I. Diku and his Five Wives   86

II. The Conflict between Ebo and Shichen   89

III. Ebo Steals Fire   89

IV. Diku's Daughters   92

Myths & Legends in the Era of Yao   97

I. The Birth of Yao   98

II. Miracles during Yao's Rule   98

III. Miracle Judge Gaoyao   100

IV. Ten Suns in the Sky and the Severe Drought   102

V. Yi Shot Suns   104

VI. Yi and Luoshen's Love Affairs   107

VII. The Legend of Hebo's Wedding   110

VIII. Chang'e Flying to the Moon   110

IX. Gun Tamed the Raging Waters   113

X. Emperor Yao's Demise   115

Myths & Legends in the Era of Shun 117

I. Birth of Shun and His Youth 118

II. Shun Ascends to the Throne 120

III. Buried at the Jiuyi Mountain 121

Myths & Legends in the Era of Dayu 123

I. The Birth of Dayu 124

II. Orders to Control the Floodwater 124

III. Dayu's Tragic Marriage 127

IV. Having all the Rivers under Control 129

Other Myths & Legends 131

I. Kuafu Chasing the Sun 132

II. Yugong Moving Mountains 134

III. Cow herd and Vega 135

Appendix 1: Major Characters in Chinese Myths & Legends 139

Appendix 2: Chronological Table of the Chinese Dynasties 143

Preface

Myths and legends have been an important part of the spiritual wealth of humankind throughout history. They are a repository of the wisdom and imagination of our ancestors; a microcosm of ancient spiritual life.

Myths tell stories of deities and heroes, the origin of the universe, how gods control the universe, how deities fight for it, the mysterious relationship between humans and deities, as well as extraordinary tales of the bravery and courage of ancient heroes. Myths touch on a wide variety of fields including ancient beliefs, morality, philosophy, science and history.

Every nation has its share of legends. In China, there were three main nationality groups in ancient times—Huaxia (Han nationality), Dongyi (Eastern Tribes) and Miaoman (Southern Tribes), which, after thousands of years, have contributed to a multifaceted Chinese nation. It is thought that Chinese mythology evolved gradually with Han tales as its core, absorbing some of the tales of the Eastern and Southern Tribes.

China's mythological history is quite different from that of Greece. First, the gods are very different. In Greek mythology, Prometheus created humans in the likeness of God; therefore, the Greek gods look exactly like human beings, and ancient sculptures of gods show perfect human bodies, such as Apollo and Aphrodite. However, in Chinese mythology, Fuxi, endowed with similar powers as Apollo, is shown as having a human head with a snake's body; so it is with Nüwa, said to be the creator of humankind.

Second, in Greek mythology humans usually cannot aspire to the status of deities, with the exception of a Hercules who rose to heaven after death and became a god.

But in Chinese mythology, the gods in Heaven and the emperors on Earth can readily trade places. The Chinese character "Di" referred to gods in ancient times, but was later also used to refer to emperors. Sacrificial offerings, such as those meant for gods, were also meant to worship emperors. In Chinese mythology the five gods in charge of the universe are Fuxi (east), Yandi (south), Shaohao (west), Zhuanxu (north) and Huangdi (center). As per legend, there are five "Dis" on Earth too, or five ancient emperors: Emperor Huangdi, Emperor Zhuanxu, Emperor Diku, Emperor Yao and Emperor Shun. Among them, Huangdi and Zhuanxu are both gods and emperors. Fuxi, Nüwa and Shennong (Yandi) were believed to be emperors on Earth in even earlier times and were respected as the "Three Emperors." Thus, the line between deities and humans in Chinese mythology is not as sharply defined as in Greek mythology. In Chinese history, there are heroes who have been worshipped as deities after their death. For example, the well-known general, Guan Yu, of the Three Kingdoms era has been worshipped as Emperor Guan or "Evil-subduing Emperor" by ordinary people, as a god of war by warriors and as the god of wealth by merchants. Influenced by a different mythological tradition and religious background, Western readers may find it difficult to understand why the Chinese worship heroes as deities. But this tradition is entrenched in Chinese culture.

The narrative structure of Chinese mythology also differs greatly from that of Greek mythology. For example, the Greeks have Zeus on top of Olympus leading the other gods in controlling the universe. But China's vast territory in ancient times was divided into three large nationalities—Han, Eastern Tribes and Southern Tribes—all of which developed their own distinctive culture. This meant there was no complete deity

Asking Heaven by the modern artist Liu Lingcang. *Asking Heaven* is a long poem by Qu Yuan (340–278 BC) of the Warring States Period (475–221 BC). It contains many stories from ancient Chinese mythology.

system with a fixed God. Furthermore, there were no epic poets such as Homer or Hesiod in China. Hence, the Chinese stories are scattered in various classical books. This, in turn, means Chinese mythology has a relatively loose narrative.

This book attempts to give readers an understanding of Chinese mythology, considering differences between traditional Chinese and Western cultures. It is hoped that this book will help readers truly appreciate these charming tales.

The Origin of the Universe

I. Chaos

The universe is vast and infinite in space and time. When primitive man pursued its origin, he tried to bring everything down to the primitive existence. Some people believe this is water, some believe it is air. The Chinese see primitive existence as chaos.

The ancient Chinese believed there was no division between heaven and earth before the birth of the universe, no light, no darkness; there was simply chaos that filled all space.

Zhuangzi, a philosopher of the Warring States Period (about 369–286 B.C.), wrote that chaos was the emperor of the central regions. Unlike men, he had no eyes, no nose, no ears and no mouth. His friends Shu, emperor of the Southern Sea, and Hu, emperor of the Northern Sea, wanted to help him by creating his seven apertures (i.e. the eyes, ears, nostrils and mouth) and so they bored these holes. They opened one for him every day and when they were done, on the seventh day, chaos died.

The death of chaos led to the birth of the universe.

II. The Beginning of the World

In Chinese legend, Pangu was the creator of all things. There are two legends about him: one, the creation of Heaven and Earth and the other, becoming all creatures on Earth after death.

It is said in Xu Zheng's *San Wu Li Ji,* written in the Three Kingdoms era, that chaos was shaped like an egg. As time passed, it gradually became pregnant with Pangu. The gestational period lasted 18,000 years and Pangu grew a huge body inside. When chaos could not bear it any more, it broke into two parts: *yin* and *yang,* the two

The *San Wu Li Ji,* or *San Wu Li,* written by Xu Zheng of State of Wu (222–280) in the Three Kingdoms (220–265) is believed to be the earliest literature recording Pangu creating the world.

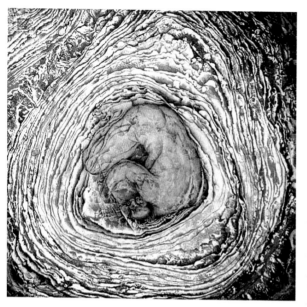

This modern oil painting illustrates Pangu's creation of heaven and earth.

opposing principles in nature. As *yang* rose high it became heaven, *yin* went down to become Earth. Pangu, standing between heaven and Earth, grew a *zhang* (more than 3 meters) every day. As he grew, heaven rose a *zhang* every day while Earth grew a *zhang* wider. Day in and day out, and year in and year out, another 18,000 years passed and Pangu grew to become a giant 90,000 *li* in height (45,000 kilometers long), which is the distance between heaven and Earth. The Pangu mythology of the creation of the universe has two main aspects to it—chaos and universe as an egg.

Another version, the *Wu Yun Li Nian Ji,* written in the same period as the *San Wu Li Ji,* describes the alteration of Pangu's body after his death. As he died, his left eye became the sun and the right eye, the moon; his hair and beard became the sky and the blinking stars; his breath became the wind and clouds, and his voice, thunder; his limbs became the four borderlines of the Earth (in ancient China, people believed the sky was round, and the Earth square), his huge trunk, the mountains; his blood, the rivers; his veins, the veins of Earth and his muscle the soil in the field; his hair became stars and planets, his skin flowers and plants; teeth and bones turned to metals and rock; semen and bone marrow, pearls and precious stones, and his sweat, rain to water and moisturize all things in the universe. Finally, the parasites on his body became primitive man.

The stories about Pangu are widespread among the Han and Zhuang nationalities. Even today, in the Tongbai Mountain area of Henan Province, there is a Pangu Mountain, on which stands an ancient temple. However, in the central Guangxi Zhuang Autonomous Region, there are Pangu Mountains, Pangu caves and a large number of Pangu temples in the Laibin, Guiping and Guigang areas. The locals in these areas still worship Pangu and pass these traditions from one generation to another.

Pangu Creates Heaven and Earth, by the modern artist Liang Qide.

Bronze statue of Pangu standing inside the Pangu Ancestral Temple in Tongbai County, Henan Province, Wu Xianlin

The Origin of Humankind

I. The Image of Nüwa

Nüwa is believed to be the creator of man, the protector of humankind and the goddess of marriage. She enjoys a high ranking and is worshipped widely. Her image is that of a snake with a human face.

On some carved stone sculptures from the Han Dynasty (206 B.C.–A.D. 220), Nüwa has two legs attached to her snake body, resembling the body of a dragon. This image of half-human and half-beast is seen often in ancient mythology. The ancient Chinese adulated the snake and adulated the dragon even more. They imagined Nüwa as a snake or dragon to denote that she was a great goddess.

Nüwa selected from *Shan Hai Jing: The Vast West*, Jiang Yinghao, Ming Dynasty (1368–1644). This image of a human head and snake body was respected in legend as a great goddess who created humanity.

However, with the development of civilization, the primitive image of Nüwa has evolved. After the Ming (1368–1644) and Qing (1644–1911) dynasties, Nüwa tended to be depicted as a woman.

II. The Creator of Human Beings

Ge Hong says in his book *Bao Pu Zi*, written in the Eastern Jin Dynasty (A.D. 317–420), that Nüwa was born on Earth. Since the Earth is believed to belong to *yin* in nature, Nüwa is seen as a goddess.

Ying Shao of Eastern Han (25–220) says in his *Annotation of Literature and Customs* that when heaven and Earth were first separated, there was no human being. Nüwa got some yellow soil, mixed it with water and made a pile of clay. With deft hands, she molded clay figurines

The two volumes of the *Bao Pu Zi* by Ge Hong (284–364), the famous Taoist scholar of the Eastern Jin Dynasty (317–420), contain many stories about deities. The *Feng Su Tong Yi* written by Ying Shao (c. 153–196) of the Eastern Han Dynasty (25–220) records a large quantity of mythological stories and legends annotated by the author. It is an important text for the study of ancient Chinese customs.

Goddess Nüwa, Liang Qide.

and empowered them with life. Nüwa became very tired after she had molded a few. So, she diluted the clay to mud, soaked a piece of rope in it and then pulled it out to wave it. Immediately, the drops of mud became women and men. Those molded carefully at the beginning became the rich and nobles, while those from mud drops became the poor and humble people.

The creation of humans with soil can be found in legends worldwide. In Greek mythology, Prometheus created humans with earth at a river bank. He molded them based on his own appearance mirrored in the water. This made humans look exactly like the gods. However, the Chinese were more inclined to the belief that a goddess created humans, perhaps because this is more in line with women giving birth to children in real life.

III. Nüwa Mending the Heaven

At the beginning of the establishment of the universe, human life was constantly under threat of collapse. Nüwa, the great mother of the human race, had to reorganize the universe.

The *Huainanzi* was compiled by Prince Liu An of Huainan (179–122 BC) in the early Western Han Dynasty (206–25). Guided by Taoist thought, it contains doctrines of various schools of thought and some mythology.

The classical Chinese text *Huainanzi* produced by Liu An, prince of Huainan, and others in the Western Han (206 B. C.–A.D. 24) period, says that in very ancient times the four poles of the Earth were destroyed, and the vast land broke up into countless valleys that made it impossible for hundreds of millions of creatures to live. Heaven broke and fell, leaving a huge black hole. Forests burnt, lighting up the universe and turning it red. Rain poured from the black hole of the collapsed heaven while black water spilled from the cracks on Earth—two raging floods that lashed the land. Bloody beasts attacked humans; fierce black birds dashed down from high above and attacked the aged and the young with their sharp claws. Humans faced extinction. At this critical moment, Nüwa brought five colored stones (in ancient times, the Chinese thought that the main five colors were blue, yellow, red, white and black), melted them and used the colorful magma to mend the black hole where heaven had been. Thus she stopped the

Goddess Nüwa Mending Heaven, Fu Tianchou. Standing in Binhai Square, Shenzhen, Guangdong Province.

On September 16, 2007, the "Nüwa Public Memorial Ceremony" was held in Mending Heaven Square in Shexian County, Hebei Province, attended by 2,000 people from all walks of life.

storm. Since Nüwa mended the heaven with colorful magma, we still see colorful clouds in the sky. Later, Nüwa repaired the Earth. She caught a huge turtle and cut off its four feet to support the four damaged poles. She collected piles of weeds, burned them and threw the ashes into the raging floods. As the ashes became thicker and thicker in the water, the floods finally stopped. With her painstaking efforts, the vast lands were pieced back together. Eventually Nüwa killed the black dragon that was threatening humans. At the death of the black dragon, all the other beasts were afraid and dared not do anything else against the people. With the protection of Nüwa, human beings once again began to lead a happy and peaceful life.

The ancient Chinese worshipped Nüwa for many generations for her glorious deeds. Before the Song Dynasty (960–1296), every year on the twenty-third of the first lunar month, people worshipped Nüwa. The day was celebrated as "Tianchuan Festival," meaning "heaven broken" festival, as that was the day Nüwa mended heaven. To remember her, on this day people made many pancakes and placed them on ceilings to imitate the way she mended heaven. Even today, in some parts of China, in the rainy season, people will tie a portrait of Nüwa to a broom and wave it, remembering how she stopped the rains.

IV. Nüwa and Marriage

Nüwa created human beings and made arrangements for them to lead a happy and peaceful life. However, she knew the limitations imposed by a single life span. To make the human race

The Bell and Drum Tower in Mending Heaven Square in Shexian County.

"Nüwa," Mending Heaven Square, Shexian County.

last forever, she created marriage. She let men and women marry so they could procreate. To celebrate this success she created *Sheng*, a musical instrument. But the word also means to give birth. *Sheng* were originally made with a gourd fixed with thirteen tubes. When blown, it would produce a melodious sound.

Thus, the ancient Chinese also respected Nüwa as "Gaomei," the Goddess of Marriage, and built a magnificent temple in her honor. Every year during spring, people, especially the young, would gather at the Hall of Gaomei to celebrate and find themselves a lover. Married couples who had no children would also join in to pray to Nüwa for a baby.

V. The End of Nüwa

There are two stories about the end of Nüwa in Chinese classics. The *Shan Hai Jing* (*Classic of the Mountains and Seas*) compiled in the Spring and Autumn and Warring States periods, says the belly of Nüwa became ten large gods named "Intestine of Nüwa." However, another book, *Huainanzi*, says that after mending heaven, Nüwa rose up to the highest part of heaven in a chariot driven by Yinglong, a winged dragon, to report to the God of Heaven and has lived there ever since.

The *Shan Hai Jing* is one of China's oldest esoteric texts, dating from the Spring-Autumn or Warring States Period. The author is unknown. It contains a large quantity of myths and legends from ancient times.

"Intestine of Nuwa" from *Shan Hai Jing: The Vast West*, Wang Fu, Qing Dynasty (1644–1911).

Universe in Myth

I. The Heaven and Earth

With the reconstruction of the universe by Nüwa, order was re-established and heaven and Earth became peaceful once more.

A boundless blue sea surrounds the four sides of the vast land—namely the East Sea, West Sea, South Sea and North Sea. The square land is located in the centre of the sea. The four poles of the Earth are firmly supported by the turtle's feet postioned by Nüwa. This brings the Earth stability and peace.

Covering the land is a boundless round sky that is divided into nine parts; each part has its own name: Juntian Sky in the center, Cangtian Sky in the east, Biantian Sky in the northeast, Xuantian Sky in the north, Youtian Sky in the northwest, Haotian Sky in the west, Zhutian Sky in the southwest, Yantian Sky in the south and Yangtian Sky in the southeast. There are altogether 9,900 corners of the sky, which is very thick and has nine layers. The highest layer is called Ninth-Layer Sky. This is the place where Nüwa meets the God of Heaven.

There are many channels linking heaven and Earth. For example, there are eight sky poles, four corners and quite a few sky ladders.

On Earth, there are eight mountains that

Two beasts guarding the Buzhou Mountain from *Shan Hai Jing: The Vast West*, Wang Fu, Qing Dynasty.

stand towering up to the sky and are referred to as sky poles. Books relating to these stories have been lost to time. We now know the names of only two of the eight poles: Mount Buzhou and Mount Kunlun—both said to have been found in northwest China. However, no one ever climbed these mountains as they were considered sacred.

The four corners - or four dimensions - are the Corner of Baode in the northeast, the Corner of Changyang in the southeast, the Corner of Beiyang in the southwest and the Corner of Titong in the northwest. A huge rope hanging from each of these corners guarantees the stability of heaven and Earth.

As the sky ladders are channels between heaven and Earth, both deities from heaven and shamans and sorcerers from the mortal world can travel between heaven and Earth via the ladders. The main sky ladder is a huge tree—Jianmu. They can also come and go between sky and Earth through the Dengbao and Lingshan mountains.

The Jianmu tree is in Duguang, the center of Earth, which is also the center of heaven. Duguang is a paradise on Earth where a variety of crops grow automatically. It is a place where lucky phoenixes and singing birds can be found, and various other mythical beasts. Huangdi, the great God of Heaven, planted the Jianmu tree himself. The tree has no branches and is simply a wobbly trunk soaring into the sky. Its leaves are dark green and very thin, while its flowers are black. Its fruit is yellow and smells like castor beans. Since it grows in the center of both heaven and Earth, it does not have a shadow when the sun shines above it at noon time. If you shout while standing under it, there will be no echo. It is a holy tree used as ladder by the gods.

Dengbao Mountain is located in a wild vast land, and is a special channel for shamans to move between heaven and Earth.

Lingshan Mountain is inside the South Sea, between Black Water River and Green Water River. Various kinds of medicinal herbs can be found on Lingshan Mountain. Since it was also home to a special kind of red snake, it was impossible for ordinary people to get close to it. However, that did not stop shamans from picking medicinal herbs in the mountains or from traveling to or from heaven and Earth.

But, the frequent traveling of the gods and shamans between heaven and Earth led to many disasters, as detailed in mythological tales. To safeguard the order of heaven and Earth, the God of Heaven destroyed the ladders and thus ended exchanges between deities and human beings.

Mythological tales of sky ladders are popular worldwide. They express the hope of human beings to overcome limitations, to live forever and savor eternal happiness. The most famous sky ladder in Western tradition is perhaps the Tower of Babel described in the Bible. Later generations of Noah planned to build a high tower, through which they could reach heaven. God was afraid that if the tower was built he would lose control over humans. So he tried to confuse them with many languages. This destroyed the communication and coordination between people and the building of the Tower of Babel failed.

II. Ten Suns and Twelve Moons

Ancient people paid special attention to celestial bodies. They believed them to be the origin of light and the origin of life. There are many mythological tales about the sun, the moon and the stars.

These include a legend from the Yin and Shang nationalities from about 3,000–4,000 years ago, about Jundi, a god who has three wives: Xihe, Changxi and Ehuang. Xihe is the mother of the suns, and Changxi is the mother of the moons.

Living outside the East Sea near Ganshui, Xihe gives birth to ten suns. She loves her suns very much and every day would

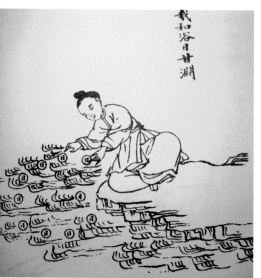

"Xihe Bathing Her Suns" from *Shan Hai Jing: The Vast South*, Wang Fu, Qing Dynasty. Xihe was the wife of Emperor Jun and the mother of the ten suns in Chinese mythology.

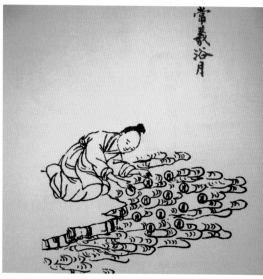

"Changxi Bathing Her Moons" from *Shan Hai Jing: The Vast West*, Wang Fu, Qing Dynasty. Changxi was also the wife of Emperor Jun and mother of the twelve moons.

bathe them in the Ganyuan waters. This made her suns' faces glow with health. Their bodies were extremely hot like fire. When they took a bath, water in Ganyuan seethed and steam rose wide and high. So, this river valley has also been referred to as a hot-water valley. After bathing, the suns would rest in a huge mulberry tree beside the river valley. The tree was about 300 *li* in height, with leaves as small as mustard seeds.

These suns of Jundi took turns to do their duty. In the morning, the sun on duty would ride his three-clawed crow and fly from east to west crossing the entire dome of the sky. At dark, he would rest at Yugu in the west of the land. Then, he would return to his mother and take another bath.

The story of the sun riding a three-clawed crow is particularly ancient, and changed during the Han Dynasty (206 BC – 220 AD). The *Huainanzi* says: Xihe, the mother, drives six dragons to pull a carriage for her son's travel through the sky. This tale is similar to the Greek mythological tale in which Phoebus Apollo drives a sun chariot every day. The chariot is pulled by four strong horses shooting flames from their mouths.

Compared with the tale about the sun, the corresponding story about the moon is incomplete. We only know that Changxi gave birth to twelve moons, she lived in vast wild land in the west and bathed her sons - moons - every day.

III. Mount Kunlun: City of Deities on Earth

In Chinese mythology deities usually live in heaven while humans live on Earth. But deities also have a place on Earth and that place is Mount Kunlun, much like Olympus in Greek mythology.

The *Shan Hai Jing* (*Collection of the Mountains and Seas*) says that Mount Kunlun, located in the vast northwest, is where the gods reside. With a circumference of 800 *li*, and a height of 8,000 *zhang*, it is also one of the eight sky poles. On the mountain top, there is a huge eight-angle rock, on which stands the palace of gods. There are five city walls and moats, and twelve palaces. The supreme God and all the other gods of the five directions, the east, west, south, north and center live in them. It has nine gates on each side, guarded by *kaiming* beasts (enlightened beasts). In addition, there are nine wells circled with jade balustrades on each of the four sides.

Mount Kunlun is rich in exotic flowers and rare herbs. *Muhe*, a sort of woody crop, is four *zhang* in height and its trunk is so thick that at least five persons linked hand-in-hand can circle it. To the east of the woody crop, are *shatang* and *langgan* trees.

Portrait of the Western Mother Goddess, Qing Dynasty.

Western Mother Goddess, carved on bricks of the Han Dynasty unearthed from Songshan Mountain in Shandong Province.

The fruit of the *shatang* tree looks like the plum but it is said that if any man eats it he can fly across a sea. The fruit of the *langgan* is actually precious pearl and jade beads, intended for the phoenixes on Mount Kunlun. The god Lizhu with three eyes and six arms lives near the *langgan* tree, protecting the fruit day and night. To the south of the woody crop is the red *jiang* tree protected by a venomous snake and a flood dragon. To the north of the woody crop, grows the most beautiful *wenyu* tree with glittering, colorful jade beads. Delicious meat, especially *shi* meat, can be found everywhere on the mountain. Shi is an animal with no limbs and bones, and is able to re-generate itself. If you eat a part of the animal, that part will grow again immediately; it can never be finished.

The two most scenic spots in the mountain are Yaochi, the abode of the Empress, and Liquan Spring with its clear and sweet water surrounded by beautiful flowers and grass.

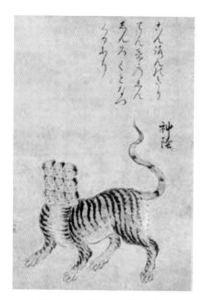

However, this magnificent mountain is not accessible to human beings. It is under the control of the god Luwu, a half-man, half-beast with a human head, tiger body and nine tails. Under him is Tulǔ, a four-horned monster, fond of eating human beings. The Qinyuan bird also likes to attack humans with its poisonous beak. There are also two obstacles on Mount Kunlun that one cannot cross—first, Ruoshui, an abyss surrounding the mountain. It is very deep, at least 240 *zhang* in depth; even a piece of the lightest feather will fall to its bottom. The second, outside the Ruoshui River, is a circle of burning mountain ranges called Yanhuo Mountain.

Luwu Beast in the *Pictures of Monstrous Birds and Beasts* published during Japan's Edo Period (1603–1868). In this picture Luwu is mistakenly named Shen Lu.

Only famous magicians, including Magician Peng, Magician Di, Magician Yang, Magician Lǔ, Magician Fan and Magician Xiang, could enter Kunlun with the permission of the gods. However, there was an exception. The hero Yi was permitted to go to Kunlun by the empress dowager of the West god because of his heroic deed of shooting suns. He became an immortal after drinking the elixirs of life the empress dowager granted him.

The *Huainanzi* says: A peak on top of Kunlun is called Cool Wind Mountain—whoever reaches there will live forever. If one passes that and continues on to Xuanpu, he will be able to summon wind and rain. Further up, he will arrive at the Palace of God and become a deity. However, this is not for ordinary humans.

IV. Deities' World in the Sea

In Chinese mythology, the land is surrounded by the sea. The ancient Chinese paid special attention to the East Sea because they were close to it, and because most of the Chinese rivers flow to the East Sea.

The ancient Chinese believed that in the east of the world there is a sea, and at the east end of that is a big crack, named Guixu (literally, returning to nothingness). Most rivers in Chinese territory flow from west to east. The well known verse "A river of spring water rolling towards the east" describes the direction of flowing water. However, although thousands of rivers flow to the sea day and night, the sea does not swell. The explanation developed by the ancient Chinese was that the water flowed into the Guixu and disappeared. This is why the seawater level remains the same.

The *Liezi*, a Taoist text produced during the Wei (220–265) and Jin (265–420) periods, says that in the East Sea there are five floating celestial mountains—Daiyu, Yuanqiao, Fanghu, Yingzhou and Penglai, separated from one another by 70,000 *li*; each is 30,000 *li* in height and at the top lies a 90,000 *li* plain. Palaces on these mountains are built with gold. Residents of these palaces are immortals who have wings so that they can fly to visit each other easily. There are forests of pearl trees and jade trees bearing delicious fruit. Whoever eats these fruits will live forever. The beasts and birds are pure white and are not stained with a single speck of dust.

The *Liezi*, thought to have been produced around the Wei (220–265) or Jin (265–420) periods, is an important Taoist classic. The text is attributed to the Taoist thinker Lie Yukou. It contains many fables, folk tales, mythology and legends.

The problem is that the five celestial mountains are not stable as they float on the sea waters. They would shake whenever a strong wind blew. The immortals did not know what to do to make the place stable and turned to the Central God Huangdi for help. Huangdi ordered Yuqiang, God of Sea, to solve the problem.

Yuqiang, grandson of Emperor Huangdi, sent fifteen huge turtles to the East Sea to support the five mountains. Three turtles were responsible for one mountain, one to carry it on its back and two to guard. They changed positions every 60,000 years. Thus the five immortal mountains became stable. Later, a giant from Longbuo State went fishing and took away six of the celestial turtles. He killed them and used their bones to practice divination. Without the support of the turtles, two mountains, Daiyu and Yuanqiao, started to float to the North Pole and finally sank in the sea. Nearly 100 million immortals lost their homes. This made Emperor Huangdi angry and he called for the destruction of Longbuo State and shortened the giants to only several meters tall.

The ancient Chinese believed that deities were sacred and difficult to approach. They did not have any special authority and never intervened in the lives of ordinary people. They were

North Sea God Yuqiang in *Shan Hai Jing: Overseas Northern*, Jiang Yinghao, Ming Dynasty. Sea God Yuqiang has a human face and a bird's body, with two black snakes twisting from his ears and red snakes at his feet. He rides two dragons when travelling.

immortals and led a life of leisure. Humans desired such a life. This explains why Chinese people have practiced austerities to learn the so-called "method for becoming immortal."

V. Capital of Ghosts and Taodu Mountain

The biggest difference between humans and deities is the immortality of the latter. After death, the spirit of man was thought to go to the Capital of Ghosts. Like death itself, the Capital of Ghosts is a terrible place for humans. The ruler is Houtu, a god subordinate to Huangdi. Houtu's body resembles an ox but his head is that of a terrifying tiger, on top of which grows a sharp horn. He has three big, blood-curdling eyes. He drives all ghosts and spirits to the abyss-of-darkness and forces them to do endless labor as punishment. There are fierce monsters there too, many of whom eat human beings.

As it is such a terrible place, ghosts and spirits do not want to go there. They would rather dangle from the edge of the universe. These wandering ghosts and spirits are administrated by Shentu and Yulei in the Taodu (literally the "Capital for the Escaped") Mountain outside the East Sea. At the summit of Taodu Mountain is a large and greenish peach tree; its peak covers a vast area of 3,000 *li*. On the peak stands a golden cock and every morning when the first sunshine casts light on Earth, it crows. At his call, the ghosts that have been wandering the whole night gather beneath the peach tree to wait to be examined by Shentu and Yulei. If any of them are found to have done bad things during the night he/she will be tied with a reed rope and thrown to Houtu. This kept the ghosts and spirits from evil behavior.

Human beings knew that these wandering ghosts were controlled by the two gods beneath the peach tree. So, when the

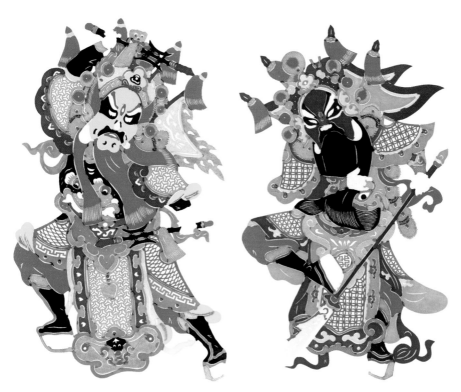

Door Gods: Shentu and Yulei.

New Year came along, they would carve the images of Shentu
and Yulei on a branch of a peach tree and hang them at their door
to drive away ghosts and spirits.

Humans have always feared death. In Greek mythology, the
nether world is ruled by Hades and is guarded by a fearsome
three-headed dog. Ghosts can enter Hades but not leave. In
Indian Buddhist tradition, there are ten kings of hell. They punish
ghosts and spirits according to what they did in the world of
humans. When Buddhism was introduced to China, the Capital
of Ghosts and the god Houtu were replaced by the Buddhist
concept of a hellish realm.

Fuxi, the God of East Heaven

I. The Birth of Fuxi

The *Liezi* says that in the remote northwest there is a country called the State of Huaxushi. It is a paradise on Earth. Though it is a country, there is no government. The people do not have desires, do not know what selfishness is and get along well with one another. They lead a long and happy life. Because of their longevity, they do not know the difference between life and death. Thus, they fear neither life nor death. To them, life and death are just the same.

One day, Huaxushi goes to Leize in the east. It is a beautiful place. Suddenly she a sees very large footprint and, curious,

The Hall of Unifying Heaven in Taihao Temple, located at the north county seat of Huaiyang, Henan Province, built for sacrifices to Taihao (Fuxi).

Thirteenth-century depiction of Fuxi.

places one of her feet in it for fun. As a result, she becomes pregnant. In fact, the footprint was left by the god Leize. Leize has a human head and dragon's body. He ruled the region with thunder and lightning. Later, Huaxushi gives birth to a boy: Fuxi.

Being the son of Leize, Fuxi's body is also half beast, half human—he has a human head and snake's body. He is very powerful. The Jianmu tree in the center of heaven and Earth is meant to be used only by gods to come and go from heaven to Earth. But, Fuxi, with mighty powers inherited from his father, climbs this sky ladder.

II. Fuxi and Nüwa: Human Creator and Goddess of Marriage

In Han Dynasty mythological tales, Fuxi and Nüwa were a couple. In some stone cuttings of this period, Fuxi is depicted having sex with Nüwa. In other images Fuxi holds a pair of compasses, symbolizing the sky, while Nüwa holds a carpenter's square resembling the square land. The first pattern symbolizes

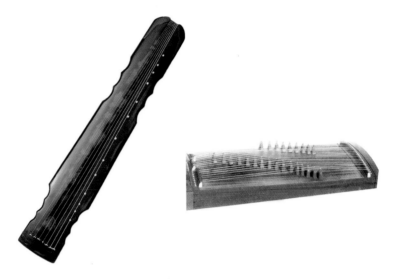

Qin and Se. Ancient Chinese stringed instruments.

human reproduction while the second one—the combination of compasses and carpenter's square—signifies the sanctity of marriage. People carve the image of Fuxi and Nüwa in ancestral tombs and ancestral halls, believing that the two who created human beings will protect the spirit of their ancestors.

As god of Marriage, Fuxi formulated the marriage system and its rites. He also invented stringed musical instruments—qin (lute) and se (psaltery).

In later mythological tales, Fuxi and Nüwa no longer appear as gods; instead they are the earliest ancestors of human beings. The *Du Yi Zhi* written by Li Kang of the Tang Dynasty (618–907), states that Nüwa and her brother Fuxi were the earliest human beings. At that time, they were the only two persons in the world. In order to reproduce, the brother and younger sister discuss marriage. However, marriage between brother and sister goes against ethical norms. They are faced with a hard choice: one is extinction of human beings, and the other, committing incest. Failing to find an answer themselves, they go to Mount

Brick carving depicting intercourse between Fuxi and Nüwa.

An image of Fuxi and Nüwa unearthed from Astana-Harahojo Ancient Cemetery in Xinjiang. It is a relic of the early Tang Dynasty (618–907). In the picture, Fuxi holds a pair of compasses in one hand and holds Nüwa by her waist with the other. The latter holds a setsquare in one hand and holds Fuxi by the waist in return. Their lower parts twist like snakes.

Kunlun to seek God's advice. Each of them makes a bonfire and prays to heaven: "Please, if we are allowed to marry, let the smoke of the two bonfires combine with one another; if not separate them." The smoke from the two bonfires rose up and mixed. This demonstrated the will of god: for humans to continue, the brother and sister should marry. And, they did. To cover her embarrassment, the sister weaves a fan with grass and covers her face. It is thought that in ancient times the bride would always hold a fan in her hand, which is a recreation of the scene when Fuxi and Nüwa married.

In another folk tale, it is said that Fuxi and Nüwa married after they survived a heavy flood. It is said that one day when Fuxi was fishing in a lake, a huge white turtle swam to him and said, "The heaven is going to fall, the Earth will sink and flood will cover the area a hundred days later. I come to your rescue, but you have to give me fish every day." Fuxi then ensures the white turtle has the requested fish every day. When the sister hears of this, she also brings fish to the white turtle. A hundred days later the disaster predicted by the turtle happens. The white turtle swallows the brother and sister and sinks deep to the bottom of the lake. In its belly the two find a palace and all the fish they have given the turtle.

When the floods recede, they emerge from the turtle and find that the entire world has changed and no one is to be found. Wondering if it is the God's will that brother and sister

Millstone.

should marry, each of them pushes a piece of millstone to the top of the mountain and prays, "Your Majesty, we are going to roll the millstones down the mountain. If you do want us to become a couple, let the upper one combine with the lower one, otherwise, we are still brother and sister." After this, each pushes the millstone down the mountain. The upper millstone combines perfectly with the lower part at the foot of the mountain and becomes a complete millstone. So, Fuxi marries Nüwa following God's instructions. They became the first ancestors of human beings.

III. Cultural Civilization of Fuxi

According to legend, Fuxi gave humankind marriage, the fishing net, fire and the Eight Diagrams used in Chinese divination.

It is said that humans did not know how to fish in ancient times. The *Shan Hai Jing* shows that primitive men caught fish by hand. After seeing spiders catching insects with the webs they produce, Fuxi learns how to weave a net with which to catch fish. In the rural areas of Zhejiang Province, people still talk about how Fuxi taught people to produce fishing nets.

The *Record of Heretofore Lost Works* was compiled by Wang Jia of the Eastern Jin Dynasty. It collects various mythological stories and rare tales from the times of Fuxi and Shennong to the Eastern Jin Period, including descriptions of the eight immortal mountains.

Fuxi also drilled wood to make fire. Since then, people have been eating cooked food, and thus distinguishing themselves from other animals. However, there is another more popular folk tale about how fire created by friction was discovered. According to *Record of Heretofore Lost Works* written by Wang Jia of the Jin Dynasty, there was once a Suiming State in the remote vast west. Even sunshine and moonlight did not reach the place and residents there could not distinguish between day and night. In this state grew a large tree, called *sui*, the branches of which stretched in all directions, covering an area of 10,000 *qing*, equal to 6.67 hectares. The tree was home to several woodpeckers. When these birds pecked at the wood, sparks would fly and this was the light by which the people lived. Later, a deity landed in this place on one of his travels and saw the sparks made by the woodpeckers. He found some hard objects with which he drilled into the wood and was finally able to make fire. Later, he returned to central China and taught people how to make fire and he is remembered with respect as Suirenshi.

In Greek mythology, Prometheus steals fire from the sacred Mount Olympus and gives it to humans in violation of Zeus' orders. Prometheus is then bound to a rock on top of Caucasus Mountains, where an eagle eats his liver every day as a punishment. Prometheus is doomed to suffer eternally since his gut re-grows even as it is eaten.

The Eight Diagrams, used by the ancient Chinese to practice divination, are considered Fuxi's most important invention. In Greek mythology, human beings ask Phoebus Apollo to predict the unknown future, while in the Chinese tradition Fuxi invents the

Sculpture of Suirenshi discovered in the tomb of Shangqiu in Henan.

Eight Diagrams to predict the future. Thus, human beings hold their future in their own hands.

Since Fuxi had super powers, the God of Heaven sent him a dragon horse to the sacred Yellow River. On the back of the dragon horse was a mysterious picture. Fuxi looked at it carefully and developed the Eight Diagrams, which has the *qian, kun, kan, li, zhen, xun, gen* and *dui* resembling respectively

"Asking Heaven Picture," Qing Dynasty. In the upper centre of the picture is a sign of Tai Ji (Great Ultimate), in the left of which is the sun and on the right the moon, represented by a three-foot bird and the legendary jade rabbit. In the lower center is a square symbolizing the regions and around it is a sign of the Eight Diagrams. The twelve animals drawn in the outside circle mark the hours of day and night.

The Fuxi Temple located in Guatai Mountain in Tianshui, Gansu Province, is said in legend to be the place where Fuxi created the Eight Diagrams.

Dragon Horse depicted in *Pictures of Monstrous Birds and Beasts* published during Japan's Edo Period.

the heaven, earth, water, fire, thunder, wind, mountain and marsh. These eight basic elements cover the entire universe and can predict the future of all creatures. Under King Wenwang of the Zhou period, the Eight Diagrams evolved into sixty-four diagrams, and was further developed into the *Yi Jing*, the greatest of ancient Chinese philosophy classics.

Fuxi is buried in Huaiyang, Henan Province. Every year there are people who go to visit his tomb and offer sacrifices to him—the first ancestor of human beings.

IV. Fuxi, the God of East Heaven

The *Huainanzi* of the Western Han period said that, after his death, Fuxi became the God of East Heaven, one of the five gods with Huangdi at the center. He governs the East Heaven with the assistance of the God of Wood, Goumang, and at the same

Stone Portrait of God of Wood, Goumang, unearthed from an Eastern Han Dynasty tomb in Shaanxi Province.

time he is also in charge of spring. He governs an entire area of 12,000 *li*, from Jieshi Mountain in Hebei Province going eastward, passing Korea and Daren State to the place where the sun rises. Since he is responsible for the east of the world and spring, Fuxi's color is green.

Yandi, the God of South Heaven

I. The Contribution of Emperor Yandi

Shaodian was a king in ancient times. His concubine Nüdeng became pregnant after intercourse with a celestial dragon. Nüdeng gave birth to a boy with a cattle head and human body: Yandi. On his birthday, nine wells appeared in the surrounding areas. Water in each of the nine wells could flow freely to any of the others.

In ancient times, humans ate grass, wild fruits, snails and freshwater mussels and often got diseases. Yandi tried to alleviate this situation. Moved by his efforts, the God of Heaven precipitates a rain of food crops. Yandi collects the seeds from heaven and sows them in the fertile fields. He invents smelting techniques and produces axes. With axes, he cuts wood to make spades and ploughs for farming. Later, he makes pickaxes with which to remove grass from the farmland. Under his guidance, people gradually grasp farming skills. Yandi has magic powers and is

Portrait of Yandi in *Collected Illustrations of the Three Realms* complied by Wang Qi and Wang Siyi of the Ming Dynasty.

able to control weather as required. Under him, people acheive bumper harvests and have enough to eat.

The ancient Chinese worshipped Yandi as emperor of farming for many generations. The Altar to the God of Farming in Beijing is the place where emperors in the Ming and Qing dynasties went to worship him. Farming was the most important part of Chinese ancient civilization. Emperor Yandi is, therefore, respected as one of the first Chinese ancestors for his contributions to developing

Sculpture of God Yandi, Yandi Cemetery in Zhuzhou, Hunan Province

God Yandi Shennong Tasted All Herbs, Liang Qide.

agriculture. Even today, every year sacrifices are made at the tomb of Emperor Yandi in Yanling County, Zhuzhou City, Hunan Province.

Yandi was also said to have used many kinds of medicinal herbs to cure the sick. It is said that his body was transparent. When he took medicine, the pharmaceutical effect in his stomach could be seen from outside. He was often poisoned by these herbs as he tried so many. At his peak, he would be poisoned as many as seventy times a day. But thanks to his celestial powers, he survived. Later, he made a magical red whip that revealed the nature of the herbs when he whipped them. He summarized his experiences in China's first medical classic

南方祝融

God of Fire, Zhu Rong, illustrated in *Shan Hai Jing: Overseas Southern*, Wang Fu, Qing Dynasty.

Goddess Yaoji, daughter of Yandi, in Wushan Mountain.

Bencao Gangmu (*Compendium of Materia Medica*). Thus Yandi is also respected as the God of Pharmacy.

II. Later Generations of Emperor Yandi

The descendants of Emperor Yandi were outstanding. The God of Fire, Zhu Rong, is his fourth generation, the God of Water, Gong Gong, his fifth, and the God of Earth Houtu, who was associated with Emperor Huangdi, is his sixth generation (though in another version Zhu Rong is the fifth generation of Emperor Huangdi).

Tingyao was the wife of Yandi and lived in Chishui River. She gave birth to Yanju. Yanju has a son named Jiebing and Jiebing's son is Xiqi. The God of Fire, Zhu Rong, with a human face and beast's body, is the son of Xiqi. When Zhu Rong goes out traveling, he rides on two dragons.

Wuxia Goddess Peak. Located in the Three Gorges of the Yangtze River, legend has it that this is the reincarnation of Goddess Yaoji.

Yandi had a daughter called Yaoji. Unfortunately, she died very young, before marriage, and became a jasper plant growing on the top of Guyao Mountain. The plant had thick leaves, beautiful golden flowers and its fruit looked like the seeds of Chinese Dodder. It was a plant of love. Yandi took pity on this daughter and conferred the title Goddess of Wushan Mountain upon her. Since then, the spirit of Yaoji can be seen in the clouds in the morning sky, while at twilight she is the rain, pouring her loneliness into lakes, rivers and the vast land. After a long time, the lonely Goddess of Wushan Mountain met King Huai of the Chu period (328–299 B.C.) in a dream and fell in love with him. When King Huai woke up he was heartbroken. Not knowing where to find her, he built a temple for the goddess to remember their brief love.

The younger daughter of Yandi was Nuwa, who was fond of playing outside. Once, when she went to play in the East Sea,

Bird Jingwei Holds a Tree Branch in the Mouth, contemporary artist Cheng Zhu.

Bird Jingwei in the *Pictures of Monstrous Birds and Beasts* published during Japan's Edo Period.

she was caught in a hurricane, swept away by waves and never returned to her beloved father. After her death, Nuwa became a little bird named Jingwei. Jingwei's body looks like a crow, but with beautiful lines on the head, a white beak and red claws. Jingwei lived in Jiushan Mountain in the north. She hated the East Sea for taking her life when she was so young and swore revenge. Every day she flew to western mountains to pick small stones and tree branches and then threw them into the sea in the hope that one day she would fill it up.

On her daily travels between the western mountains and East Sea, Jingwei gets to know Haiyan, a sea swallow, and they marry. They have numerous offspring; the female birds look like Jingwei while the males look like Haiyan.

III. Chaos in Emperor Yandi's Era

It is said that at the end of the Yandi period, social morality declined and some states began to invade one another; they took away farmlands, grabbed properties and people. Yandi had to declare war against these states. Later, Emperor Huangdi conquered Yandi and restored peace. Some stories maintain that Yandi was killed by Huangdi, and others claim that he fled to the south. The *Huainanzi* says that eventually Yandi became the God of the South and governed the universe together with the Central God Huangdi.

With the God of Fire, Zhu Rong, Yandi is responsible for summer and governs an entire area of 12,000 *li*, in both heaven and Earth in the south, from Beihusun southward to the South Pole. Since he is responsible for the south and summer, Yandi's color is red.

Emperor Huangdi, the God of Central Heaven

I. The Birth of Emperor Huangdi

Legend has it that in ancient times a girl named Fubao was struck by lightning. It was midnight and the dazzling lightning illuminated the Earth. Fubao was impregnated by the lightning and after twenty-five months gave birth to Emperor Huangdi in Shouqiu (today's Qufu in Shandong Province). As his birth is caused by lightning, he is regarded as the god of thunder and rain.

Another tale says that Emperor Huangdi was born to Youjiao, the wife of Shaodian. He spoke as soon as he was born, and was very intelligent. When he grew up he became the leader of his people.

Xuanyuan Emperor Huangdi.

II. The War between Emperor Huangdi and Emperor Yandi

When Emperor Huangdi assumed power, he was faced with an extremely chaotic situation. Huangdi had to organize armies and also train different kinds of wild animals to strengthen his power.

Emperor Huangdi and Yandi are thought to have had a bloody war in Banquan (within the boundaries of Shanxi or Hebei provinces). Yandi used fire to attack Huangdi, while the latter

Stone carving of Emperor Huangdi in the Xuanyuan Temple in Huangling County, Shanxi Province.

depended on thunderstorms. Huangdi commanded tigers, leopards, wolves and bears to fight on earth, while eagles and vultures made-up the air strike. It was a fierce fight. After three confrontations, Huangdi vanquished Yandi. He established his capital city, Youxiong, in today's Xinzheng, Henan Province.

III. War between Emperor Huangdi and Chiyou

In Chinese mythology Chiyou is an evil god with a bull's head and a human body. He has hard, sharp horns on his head and blade-like hairs on his ears. He has eighty-one brothers, all of

Chiyou carved on stone by Han Dynasty artists.

Chiyou.

whom are half-man, half-beast. The top of their heads is made of copper and their foreheads of iron. Chiyou and his brothers are ferocious and eat sand and stones. Chiyou invents many kinds of weapons, including the lance, arrow and shield. This makes his army extremely formidable in battle and he frequently attacks other countries.

Chiyou was a subject of Yandi, and possibly fought in the war between Yandi and Huangdi in Banquan. After Yandi was defeated, he was handed over to Huangdi, and temporarily given the title God of War. When Emperor Huangdi convened a conference of gods in west Mount Taishan, Chiyou attended. At that time, Emperor Huangdi travelled on a precious vehicle pulled by elephants and driven by the one-footed, human-faced Bifang bird; six dragons fly just behind the vehicle, which is followed closely by a troop of gods. The God of War, Chiyou,

The fresco in Xuanyuan Pavillion in Henan Xinzheng Primogenitor's Mountain depicts the war between Emperor Huangdi and Chiyou.

walks in front of Emperor Huangdi's vehicle, leading a crowd of tigers, leopards and wolves to clear the way.

However, Chiyou eventually launched a rebellion. First, he mobilized his eight-one copper-head and iron-forehead brothers, then enlisted ghosts, evil demons and monsters living in woods, mountains, rivers and lakes, and finally forced the Miao people in the south to attack Emperor Huangdi. Despite being faced with sudden chaos, Emperor Huangdi did not show any weakness and led Yinglong, Fenghou and the other gods to do battle in Zhuolu, Hebei Province, just beside Banquan.

Since Chiyou was fully prepared for war and all the gods, ghosts and giants he led were intrepid, they won a number of battles in the beginning. Furthermore, as a war-god, Chiyou is skilled in fighting; he can control the forces of nature, blow smoke and create fog. Using this strong fog, he was able to surround Emperor Huangdi and all his troops who were not able to distinguish clearly the direction. As a result, Huangdi and his troops were routed.

But Fenghou, a subordinate of Emperor Huangdi, stood out. He used a magnet to invent a south-pointing chariot and erected a statue of God on the vehicle. No

Southward pointing cart.

matter what direction the vehicle revolved, the statue always pointed south. Under the guidance of the south-pointing chariot, Emperor Huangdi and his army broke the tactical deployment of fog, and continued fighting.

Chiyou has a subordinate called Chimei, a monster with the body of a beast and the face of a child. He has long ears, red eyes, black hairs and four feet. His body is black and red. Though he is very short, he is good at puzzling others with clever words. Chimei and other ghosts use black magic unceasingly in the battlefield to confuse the enemy. However, one of Huangdi's subordinates blew a cow-horn, very vigorously, which resounded throughout the entire battlefield. This lifted the black magic completely. Emperor Huangdi launched counter attacks, and finally won the battle.

Nuba in *Shan Hai Jing: The Vast North*, Wang Fu, Qing Dynasty.

Chiyou then began to prepare for another battle. He invited Fengbo and Yushi, who govern wind and rain respectively, to join him. The God of Wind, Fengbo, has a deer body and bird head, with a pair of sharp horns on it; his tail looks like a snake with many veins. The God of Rain, Yushi, is as tiny as a silkworm egg. Both Fengbo and Yushi were subordinates of Emperor Huangdi, but in this battle, they moved over to the side of Chiyou and fought against Huangdi.

As soon as they arrived at Zhuolu, Fengbo and Yushi launched violent storms. Though Yinglong, subordinate of Emperor

Huangdi, can control rain, he was useless against Fengbo and Yushi. The violent storm forced Huangdi and his troops to scatter in all directions.

Emperor Huangdi has no idea what to do. He has to go to heaven and ask his daughter for help. Ba, daughter of Huangdi, is an ugly, bald woman. As soon as she arrived at the battlefield, wrapped in black, Ba started to discharge blazing rays of light from her bald head. The violent storm disappeared at once; the rain on the ground dried up. Fengbo, Yushi and Chiyou were helpless to prevent victory slipping from their grasp.

Emperor Huangdi then killed a one-footed monster and denuded his skin to make a war drum. He also killed a thunder beast (it is said that the thunder beast likes hitting his belly to make a thundering sound), and used his bones to make drumsticks. Huangdi beat the drum with the drumsticks, and made a sound even louder than the clap of thunder. This cheered Huangdi's troops, and frightened Chiyou and his subordinates.

Tomb of Chiyou in today's Nanwang Township, Wenshang County, Shandong.

Yinglong then killed many of Chiyou's brothers, and a giant who had come to help Chiyou in the battle. All the other rebels escaped. But Yinglong did not give this chance to Chiyou and captured him in the battlefield.

Chiyou was taken to Emperor Huangdi in fetters and killed in Zhuolu. The *Shan Hai Jing* says that at the time of the execution Huangdi's subordinates feared that Chiyou would use his celestial powers and escape. So they did not remove his fetters. When Chiyou was killed, his thick blood spilled on the wooden fetters. The subordinates threw the fetters into the wilderness where they immediately turned into a maple forest. All maple-tree leaves are bloody red, like the blood of Chiyou.

There is another story about the spot where Chiyou was killed. It is said that after Chiyou lost the war in Zhuolu, he continued to fight. Emperor Huangdi, leading his troops, chased him up to Shanxi, where Chiyou was killed. Later, the location of Chiyou's death was called "Xie" (now, Xie County in Shanxi Province). When Chiyou was killed, his blood poured out and formed a lake - the red Xie pool. The Xie pool was a famous salt lake in ancient China. In the Song Dynasty, it covered 120 *li*. Legend had it that it was Chiyou's blood that made the water red.

Emperor Huangdi held a huge victory celebration. All the deities came to congratulate him. The god of silk also came from the remote northern wildness, wearing a horse skin. She presented a piece of bright and beautiful silk to Emperor Huangdi, who wrote a melody, "Melody of Drum," to celebrate the victory. It included ten movements, that is: Astonishment of Thunder, Fierce Tiger, Eagle Pecking, Dragon Dancing, Deities Roaring, Vulture and Fish Hawk Fighting, The Rise of Hero, Roaring of Bear, Stone Flying and Wave Sweeping. The melody recreates the battlefield scene. Order returned to the cosmos and peace to Earth.

Although Emperor Huangdi won the war, he paid a high price. His beloved daughter Ba lost most of her divine power during the battle, and so could not return to heaven. But, wherever she lives, she brings a heavy drought. Frustrated by this, people send the deity of the field, Shujun, to Huangdi. Huangdi was helpless and had to send Ba to a stretch of Mount Kunlun.

Yinglong in *Shan Hai Jing: The Vast East*, Hu Wenhuan, Ming Dynasty.

But Ba likes traveling and often comes down from the mountain and, as a result, caused drought frequently in the north. The locals despised her and whenever a drought occurred, they dug a drain and implored Ba to return to her own land.

Furthermore, Yinglong, the beloved subordinate of Emperor Huangdi, also suffered from the aftereffects of war and could not go back to heaven. He stayed in southern China and, since he is a dragon, there is always rain in the south.

IV. Xingtian Scrambles for the Throne

After Emperor Huangdi defeated Emperor Yandi and Chiyou, the entire cosmos became calm. However, occasionally fights broke out. For example, Xingtian once attempted to take the throne.

In Chinese mythology, Xingtian, who used to be a subordinate of Emperor Yandi, is full of artistic talent. On the orders of Emperor Yandi, he once composed a melody called "Plough," in praise of agriculture. He also wrote a poem "Bumper Harvest" as a prayer for a good harvest year. Xingtian was a powerful general. After Emperor Yandi was defeated, Xingtian was not willing to obey Emperor Huangdi, and so fought against him for the throne in the state of Jigong in the west. With a shield in one hand and a big ax in the other, he fought against Emperor Huangdi alone. But although he was strong and powerful, he was no match for Huangdi, and is killed. Fearing his resurrection, Huangdi

Xingtian in *Shan Hai Jing: Overseas Western*, Bi Yuan, Qing Dynasty.

buried his head in Changyang Mountain, far away from where his body was buried. As expected, Xingtian did not give up easily. Failing to find his head, he took his two nipples as eyes and his navel as a mouth. Brandishing a shield and ax, he roars indignantly to the sky.

The expression, "rather die than surrender" is commonly used in China to laud those with a strong will. However, Xingtian went one better —"He perseveres even after death." Tao Yuanming (365–427), a poet of the East Jin Dynasty, praised Xingtian with such words as: "Xingtian looks upon his death like a game; his fierce ambition will never die."

V. The Daily Life of the Central God Huangdi

It is said that Emperor Huangdi assigned five gods of heaven, including himself, to govern the universe. He asked Luwu to manage Mount Kunlun, the earth god Houtu to take charge of the capital of Youdu and the ocean god Yuqiang to anchor the five celestial mountains in the middle of the sea; no one dared to defy his order. For the gods' convenience, Emperor Huangdi planted a Jianmu tree in between heaven and earth, so that the gods and deities could move between the two realms.

Emperor Huangdi arbitrates in all disputes among the deities. Since he is very fair and just, he wins the respect of all.

However, Gu, son of the God of Mount Zhongshan, killed the deity Baojiang, together with the celestial Qinpei in the south of Mount Kunlun. Huangdi was furious when he discovered this criminal act. He caught the two murderers, and sentenced them to death in the east side of Mount Zhongshan. Qinpei became an eagle, with a hoary head, red beak and tiger claws; whenever he appears on Earth, a war is certain to take place. Gu became a strange bird, looking like an owl, with a hoary head, a straight beak and red claws; wherever he appears, a terrible drought occurs.

At another time, the god Erfu with his snake body and human face killed the god Yayu, at the instigation of his subordinate Wei. Emperor Huangdi tied up their hands with their hair, locked their feet with fetters, and fastened them to the big tree on Shushu Mountain. The two were ravaged by wind, storm and snow. Huangdi then sent someone to move Yayu's corpse to the top of Mount Kunlun and asked six sorcerers to give Yayu immortality pills and bring him to life. After Yayu was revived, he expressed his gratitude to Emperor Huangdi and decided

Wei, subordinate of Erfu, tied to a huge tree on Shushu Mountain by Emperor Huangdi, *Shan Hai Jing: Domestic Western*, Jiang Yinghao, Ming Dynasty.

to pay him back. He jumped into the Ruoshui River at the foot of Mount Kunlun and ate anyone who dared to try to cross to invade heaven.

With peace restored, Emperor Huangdi is finally able to enjoy his life in the celestial palace. He often leaves Mount Kunlun and travels. He goes frequently to Qingyao Mountain, governed by the goddess Wuluo. Wuluo has a human face but also leopard spots, snow-white teeth, a slender waist and gold earrings. When she walks, she looks very graceful and attractive, with all her ornaments swaying and jingling. Qingyao Mountain is a place that women wish to go to. The plants there have rectangular stems and blooming yellow flowers and produce a red fruit which, when eaten by a woman, will make her beautiful forever. There is also a special kind of green bird with pink eyes and red tail that resembles a duck. Eating the meat of this bird will help a woman get pregnant.

Not far from Mount Kunlun stands Mishan Mountain, another favorite of Emperor Huangdi. Mishan Mountain abounds in a kind of soft white jade; jade cream, very smooth with a sweet scent, oozes from this jade. Huangdi eats jade cream every day, and with the leftovers, waters the *danmu* tree (red wood). Five years later, the *danmu* tree blooms with five-color flowers and produces delicious, five-flavored fruit. Later, Huangdi moves some of the white jade to Zhongshan Mountain. Thus, Zhongshan Mountain also starts to produce beautiful jade and the deities that live on Zhongshan eat the jade. Thus humans wear ornaments of white jade to ward off evil spirits.

Since gods and spirits often eat jade in Chinese mythology, when people tried to attain immortality in ancient times they ate food mixed with jade powder.

VI. The Contributions of Emperor Huangdi and his Subordinates

Many great inventions are attributed to Emperor Huangdi and his subordinates.

Legend has it that in ancient times human beings led a life similar to animals. They lived in natural caves and were at the mercy of wild beasts. Later, a sage named Youchaoshi, inspired by birds' nests, built a dwelling in a tree. Thus, humans began

Stamps issued in 2000 commemorate the ceremony of sacrificing to ancestors in Emperor Huangdi's hometown. The stamp illustrations reflect the noble deeds of the ancient Emperor.

to live in the trees, just like birds. But living in trees was not at all convenient. Emperor Huangdi took the lead and constructed houses on the ground, starting a new age.

Emperor Huangdi also invented traps to catch wild beasts so that human beings had enough meat to eat. Yongfu, a minister under Huangdi, invented the pestle, which is used for removing the husks of grain; Huangdi then invented the pot, which was used to cook rice. Boyu, also a minister under Emperor Huangdi, created clothing, which helped humans shelter from wind and rain and the cold. Emperor Huangdi invented a vehicle for personal use and thus improved transportation.

But the most outstanding invention was that of Cangjie. Cangjie has four eyes, all discharging rays of light and showing supreme intelligence. By observing the circular wavy lines of the Kui Star in the sky, studying the shape of the Earth, mountains and valleys, the patterns on a tortoise's back, and the footprints of birds, Cangjie finally invented the Chinese characters that are still being used today. When this news spread to heaven, the God of Heaven began to worry about human beings taking advantage of the creation of characters. Therefore, the God of Heaven sent down a rain of millet, warning humans not to abandon crop production, and thus avoid starvation in the future. The ghosts on earth also feared the invention of characters. They worried about human beings reporting

The portrait of Canjie in Kuixing Building, Chengde, Hebei Province.

their crimes to heaven and could not help crying loudly. The quiet night is filled with doleful sounds. Since Cangjie invented characters, Emperor Huangdi assigns him to be officer of history, and puts him in charge of historical records.

Leizu, the wife of Emperor Huangdi, is the first person engaged in raising silkworms.

The art of raising silkworms starts with the story of the Goddess of Silkworms. In ancient times, a father leaves home on a long journey, and is gone for many years. Waiting at home alone, his daughter misses him very much. One day, she speaks to her horse as she feeds him: "Dear horse, if you are able to bring my father back, I'll marry you." The horse immediately breaks loose and rushes out of the door. No one knows how long it runs; finally the horse reaches her father. The man is surprised when he sees the horse. He begins to worry about his daughter's safety, and so he rides the horse to return home. The father and daughter are very happy to see each other after so many years. The father asks whether there is something wrong at home. The daughter says that everything is fine, except for his absence. And now, the horse has brought him back. The father thinks that the horse is very clever, so he feeds it with the best foods. But the horse has no interest in the food; it just stares at the daughter. Whenever the daughter passes by the horse, it roars, jumps and kicks.

Finally, the father notices the abnormal behavior of the horse and asks the daughter quietly: "Why does the horse make such a noise upon seeing you?" The daughter cannot hide the truth and tells her father what she promised to the horse. The father is very angry and says, "What a shameful thought." Although he likes the horse very much, he cannot bear the thought of it marrying his daughter. He takes a bow, shoots the horse, denudes its skin and dries it in the sun.

One day, when the father is not home, the daughter invites a neighbor's daughter to play with her in the yard. When she sees the horse skin on the ground, she tramples on it and says angrily, "You beast, you wanted to marry a human! Now, you are dead. It serves you right." As soon as she utters these words, the horse skin suddenly flies up, wraps around her tightly and carries her afar. The neighbor's daughter rushes to find the father and tells him what happened. For several days, the father and other villagers search for the daughter and finally locate her in a big mulberry tree. However, she and the horse skin have changed into a huge silkworm. The silkworm shakes its head slowly to produce white shining silk. In the end, it makes a very thick cocoon, and wraps itself completely. Later, it becomes the Goddess of Silkworms; the image of which is a girl covered in a horse skin.

When Emperor Huangdi celebrates his victory in the war against Chiyou, the Goddess of Silkworms presents bundles of silks to Huangdi. He orders people to weave them into fabric and use the fabric to make ceremonial wear. Leizu, the empress of Huangdi, shows great interest in silk. She inquires about how it is made and starts to raise silkworms herself. The silk produced by the silkworms Leizu raises are as beautiful as those presented by the Goddess of Silkworms. Ever since, the rearing of silkworms and silk weaving have become important occupations for women.

Being the earliest woman to raise silkworms, Leizu is worshiped as "Silkworm-Raising Goddess" in China. Every spring in feudal times, when the Chinese emperor imitated the God of Farming and held a ceremony of cultivation, the empress would imitate Leizu, and hold a silkworm-raising ceremony.

The Goddess of Silkworms, Liang Qide.

In Chinese mythology, Fuxi, Nüwa and Emperor Yandi all contributed inventions; however, Emperor Huangdi is credited with the most and is regarded as the pioneer of Chinese civilization. Locals in Xinzheng, Henan, native place of Huangdi, and Huangling, Shaanxi, where Huangdi's mausoleum is located, held various kinds of rituals annually to pay tribute to Emperor Huangdi's great achievements.

The mausoleum of Emperor Huangdi is located in Huangling County, Shaanxi.

The Sacrificial Pavilion in the mausoleum of Emperor Huangdi.

Shaohao, the God of West Heaven and Zhuanxu, the God of North Heaven

I. Shaohao in Chinese Myth

Shaohao, also named Zhi, is not only a remote emperor of ancient Chinese legend, but also the God of West Heaven and Mountain Deity.

During the era of Huangdi, a huge star with a colorful tail flies across the sky and falls on Huazhu Island. Just at that moment, a young woman, Nüjie, is dreaming about making love with a man. Then, she finds that she is pregnant. Later, she gives

Shaohao.

birth to a baby: Shaohao. On the day of his birth, many phoenixes dance in the sky to celebrate. Because this happened during the period of Huangdi, then the Central God of Heaven, and a falling star and phoenix are all symbols associated with an emperor, it is said that Shaohao is the son of Emperor Huangdi.

Another story says that Shaohao is the son of Venus. Fairy Huang'e flies into the Palace of Heaven at night, and travels on a raft during the day. One day, she arrives at the shore of the West Sea and sees a big mulberry tree which is 800 *zhang* in length. Its leaves are bright red and the mulberries purple black. It was said that this kind of mulberry produced fruit at an interval of 10,000 years and that if a human ate them, he would never die. Because of the tree, the place is called Qiongsang (Extreme Mulberry). Huang'e likes the place and so stops her raft there and enjoys herself. Just at that moment, Venus changes into a handsome young man and arrives at the waterside. He plays a psaltery and sings for her. Since his psaltery is made of *wenzi* wood, it gives out a very beautiful sound. Huang'e is lured by the handsome young man and wonderful music. She invites him to her raft. The man sits beside Huang'e and plays his psaltery continuously while Huang'e sings a beautiful song of love. The two make love and Shaohao is their son.

Shaohao becomes an emperor when he grows up, and makes Qiongsang the capital city. Later, he becomes the deity of Changliu Mountain. This mountain is very beautiful; all the wild animals have pretty tails, and the birds have beautiful patterns on their crowns. The mountain is also rich in jade. Shaohao builds his palace on the mountain top and rules the area. Since it is located in the west, every day at sunset, Shaohao would use the afterglow of the setting sun to create a reflection to the east.

When Shaohao sees Guixu, a huge rift valley at the edge of the East Sea, he likes it very much and founds another kingdom named the State of Shaohao. To commemorate the dancing phoenixes that appeared at his birth, he makes all the birds his

The phoenix, king of the birds in Chinese mythology, is an auspicious sign.

officials. For example, the phoenix is put in charge of the calendar; swallows, quails and golden pheasants govern the seasons; the powerful and strong vultures are the army officials; the impartial and incorruptible eagle takes charge of laws; the

The stone memorial archway in the Mausoleum of God Shaohao in Shangdong Qufu.

The grave of Shaohao in Shandong Qufu.

pigeon is assigned to administer education because it shows great respect for its parents, while being strict to its wife. The five kinds of pheasants are put in charge of construction, smelting, chinaware, leather goods and dyeing respectively. The State of Shaohao is simply a state of birds. His nephew Zhuanxu, the future God of North Heaven, grows up there. Shaohao gives him a lute and psaltery, thinking that the young man would like them. However, although Zhuanxu likes listening to music, he does not like to play it himself and throws away the musical instruments. He likes power and often helps Shaohao deal with state affairs.

Shaohao has many children, some of whom are virtuous, and others evil. One of his sons named Zhong becomes the God of Wood, Goumang, and assists the god of East Heaven, Fuxi. Another son is called Rushou, his assistant. Qiongqi is an evil son of Shaohao, a bear with a tiger's body and wings. He often eats humans. He does not like his father's control and so escapes to the north. There, he runs even wilder. If he encountered a conflict between two people, he would always kill and eat the one who was innocent and just; he would bite the nose of faithful men and give wild animals to evil men as presents.

In historical tales passed down from ancient times, Shaohao is an emperor on Earth. He makes Qufu in Shandong Province the capital city of his state, and is buried there. The Shaohao Mausoleum in Qufu was built in the Song Dynasty. It is the only mausoleum built in the pyramid style in China.

During the Han Dynasty, people believed that Shaohao became the God of West Heaven after his death, where his son Rushou assisted him. The two are responsible for autumn and govern an entire area of 12,000 *li*, both heaven and Earth in the west, from the West Pole stretching eastward to across the Mount Kunlun. Shaohao's color is white.

II. Birth of Zhuanxu

Zhuanxu is the grandson of Emperor Huangdi (or great grandson in another tale), son of Changyi and nephew of Shaohao. His mother is Jingpu. At the end of Shaohao's period, a peculiar omen appears in the sky: the Yaoguang Star of the Big Dipper suddenly runs across the moon. Jingpu, imperial concubine of King Changyi, who lives in the Palace of Youfang, is impregnated by the Yaoguang Star. Later, when King Changyi is banished to the riverside

Emperor Zhuanxu.

of Ruoshui River in the southwest, Jingpu follows him and delivers Zhuanxu there. The baby is born carrying a shield and dagger, indicating that he would face wars and win them with force.

Zhuanxu is very clever. He is able to assist Shaohao when he is only ten years old. He looks like an adult at twelve and becomes emperor at twenty. He makes Diqiu (today's Puyang of Henan Province) his capital city. To guarantee the peace of the state, he often rides a dragon to make his rounds and visits all the areas where sunshine reaches. After his return, he

Emperor Zhuanxu in the Two Emperors Mausoleum in the Huangxian County in Henan.

orders the Flying Dragon to imitate the wind of the different areas and composes music based on it. A melody entitled "Chengyun" (Clouds) is composed specially for the Central God of Heaven, Huangdi.

III. Cutting off the Link between Heaven and Earth

Emperor Huangdi adores Zhuanxu. He even lets him govern the universe on his behalf. Seizing this opportunity, Zhuanxu begins to cut the link between heaven and Earth.

By this time, gods and deities from the heaven and shamans from the Earth can go to and from heaven and Earth constantly, via the sky ladders and poles. However, some evil gods and spirits, such as Chiyou, take advantage of the situation and make trouble. Although Chiyou is killed, the once peaceful universal order is destroyed and Huangdi's daughter Ba and his subordinate Yinglong are seriously hurt in war and cannot return to heaven.

Zhuanxu convinces himself that the constant travel between heaven and Earth is full of latent dangers. He also fears that the wars launched by Chiyou might surface again sometime in the future. To prevent this from happening, he decides to cut off all links between the celestial and human world. He sends two gods, Zhong and Li, to carry out the task.

To separate the poles and ladders between heaven and Earth, Zhong uses his mighty power to prop up the heaven, and at the same time Li presses down hard on the earth with his two hands. Pressing and propping, the two gods make the distance between heaven and earth grow ever larger until finally the original ladders and poles cannot reach heaven. This leads to the creation of two worlds—a heaven for the gods and an Earth for humans. Gods cannot travel to Earth at their will, nor can humans go to heaven. Zhuanxu also orders Zhong to take charge of heaven, and Li of Earth.

For a long time after, the universe is quiet and Zhuanxu feels satisfied with what he has done. Soon, he begins to think he can do whatever he wants. He changes the cosmic order arbitrarily and tyrannizes the other gods. The wildest thing he does is to fix the sun, moon and stars on the north sky, and stop them from moving. As a result, some areas have plenty of sunshine while in other parts people are plunged into total darkness. All creatures suffer greatly from the tyranny of Zhuanxu.

IV. War Between Zhuanxu and Gonggong

Zhuanxu's tyranny finally triggers a revolt from Gonggong and his followers.

Gonggong is the son of the God of Fire Zhu Rong and the fifth grandson of the God of South Heaven, Emperor Yandi. He holds the position of deity of water and has a human head, hands and feet but a snake's body. In addition to crops, he eats all kinds of beasts. Gonggong has two followers, Xiangliu, and Fuyou. Xiangliu has nine heads, a human face and a black snake's body. His nine heads can move individually, and he must go to nine mountains to feed the nine heads. As soon as he passes a place, it turns into a swamp. Xiangliu and Fuyou, who becomes a large red bear after his death, assist Gonggong in controlling all the rivers.

Zhuanxu did not realize that Gonggong would try to usurp his throne. He leads his subordinate God of Sea Yuqiang, to fight against Gonggong.

This is the largest war since Emperor Huangdi's defeat of Chiyou. Since both Zhuanxu and Yuqiang have magical powers, they are gradually able to control the wind. When Gonggong is no longer able to ward off the blows, he retreats to a place near a big mountain in the wild northwest. The mountain was one of the eight heaven pillars, soaring into the sky. Gonggong realizes he is losing and cannot control his indignation. He wants to perish together with Zhuanxu, so he throws himself at the mountain. The mountain cannot bear his weight and breaks into two. Hence, the mountain is later called Buzhou Mountain, which means "broken one."

The *Huainanzi* says that after Gonggong flings himself at the mountain, the sky loses support in the

Gonggong throws himself at the mountain in indignation.

northwest and collapses. The sun, moon and stars that have been fixed in the north sky are freed as the sky caves in. They move northwestward and resume the normal circular track from east to west. The instant when Gonggong flung himself at the mountain, he also broke the rope linking heaven and Earth. When the rope breaks, the southeastern part of the Earth sinks. As a result, most of the rivers in Chinese territory flow toward the southeast.

The stable cosmic system under Zhuanxu's domination is destroyed by Gonggong. After this, no god renovates it, and the universe enters a new age that continues to the present day.

Gonggong hides in a pool after losing the war and his subordinates scatter in different directions.

V. The Origin of the Mengshuangshi Tribe

Zhuanxu attached great importance to the legal system and punished all immoral acts.

It is said that once a man falls in love with his sister, which greatly angers Zhuanxu. He banishes them to the remote woods of Kongtong Mountain in the west. There is nothing to eat there and nowhere to live. The brother and sister suffer from hunger and cold. They have nothing to do but hug each other tightly to resist the cold and eventually they die. When a deity bird flies over and sees this miserable scene, she drops some grass on their bodies. After seven years they come alive, but grow into one who has two heads, four arms, four legs but one trunk. Their children also have this appearance. As the time goes by, more generations come into existence, and finally form a tribe called Mengshuangshi (double-body clan).

The story of the Mengshuangshi tribe reflects the extreme fear in ancient times of the consequences of committing incest.

VI. The End of Zhuanxu

There are three stories about the ancient Emperor Zhuanxu's mausoleum. One says that Zhuanxu is buried on the south side of the Wuyu Mountain in the north. His nine imperial concubines are buried on the north side of the mountain slope. The mausoleum is guarded by ferocious animals such as bears

Zhuanxu Rides a Dragon, Qicheng Site Park in Henan Puyang.

and tigers. Another story says Zhuanxu's mausoleum is in Huangxian Country, Anyang City in Henan Province. And yet another says his mausoleum is in Liaocheng, Shandong Province. According to legend, Zhuanxu's birthday falls on the eighteenth of the third month of the lunar calendar. Even today, people celebrate his birthday and conduct many rituals to mark this occasion.

During the Han Dynasty, people believed that after his death Zhuanxu became the God of North Heaven with the deity of the sea, Xuanming, helping him. Zhuanxu is responsible for winter and governs an area of 12,000 *li*, both in heaven and on Earth in the north, from Jiuze to the North Pole. His color is black.

VII. The Offspring of Zhuanxu

Zhuanxu has many children. His son Laotong becomes the God of Heaven and Qiongchan, the Kitchen God. His other three sons die early and become ghosts and monsters who bring disease to the human world: one lives in Changjiang River, and brings on the plague; one lives in Ruoshui River, and becomes a monster; one lives in the houses of humans and frightens babies. Another of Zhuanxu's sons develops strange characteristics. He likes to be in rags, eats the remains of others and looks skinny. On a cold winter night, he starves to death in an alleyway, and is transformed into a poor ghost. People who meet him end up leading a poor life. This is the reason that the ancient Chinese would hold a ceremony at the end of the first lunar month, to "see the poor ghost off."

Zhuanxu's offspring established many states, such as the State of Jiyu, State of Zhuanxu, State of Shushi and State of Shuchu.

Myths in the Era of Emperor Diku

I. Diku and his Five Wives

The prototype of Diku is the God of Heaven Dijun, worshiped during the Shang Dynasty (sixteenth-eleventh century B.C.), and father of the ten suns and twelve moons. With the destruction of the dynasty, stories about him die out and in tales Dijun is changed to Diku—an emperor on Earth in ancient times.

It is said that Diku is the son of Zhuanxu and great grandson of Huangdi. Diku is very clever. He is able to help his father Zhuanxu at fifteen and is made king of a state as reward for his meritorious deeds. He is the successor of his father Zhuanxu and becomes Emperor Diku. He has five wives—Zoutushi, Jiandi, Jiangyuan, Qingdu and Changyi.

After Huangdi wipes out Chiyou, he moves the ordinary people to a place called Zoutu State. Its people adopt the name of the state as their own and call themselves Zoutushi. In Zoutu State lives a magical girl, who is able to fly, riding the wind and clouds. She likes the landscapes around the Yihe and Luohe rivers in the central plains and often flies there. Diku falls in love with this young lady and meets her often at the river bank. Later, he marries her. After marriage, Zoutushi often dreams that she has eaten a sun and after every such dream she gives birth to a boy. Altogether she has eight such dreams and gives birth to eight sons. All eight have enormous power and become gods in charge of all aspects of agriculture.

Emperor Diku

Diku's second wife is Jiandi, daughter of Yousongshi. One day, Jiandi and her younger sister are having a meal on top of a platform. Diku sends a swallow to lure them. The swallow flies up and down and sings above the head of the two girls. The girls cannot help trying to catch it with a jade basket. It is not easy, but finally they manage to trap it under the basket. However, when they put their hands inside the basket to catch it, it flees. Disappointed, Jiandi moves the basket away and finds two bird's eggs left inside. She is curious about them, and eats one. As a result, she becomes pregnant and gives birth to a boy named Xie. Xie becomes the forefather of the Shang nationality when he grows up.

Jiangyuan is the daughter of Youtaishi. Once, when she is out sightseeing, she finds a huge footprint on the way. She has never seen a footprint that big, and, curious, puts one of her feet in it. She then feels a shaking in her heart. Soon after she returns, she discovers that she is pregnant. She gives birth to a round flesh ball. When she sees this strange thing, she is very frightened. Quietly, she throws it into a quiet, narrow lane. Just then, a flock of sheep and cattle go to the lane. Jiangyuan notices that as the animals pass by the flesh ball they keep away from it and are afraid to hurt it. She has to pick it up again and wants to throw it into a forest. However, she finds a group of workers felling trees and there is no way she can leave it there. Finally, she hardens her heart and throws it on a frozen surface of a desert pool. Suddenly, a large bird flies down from the sky and lands on the ice. It opens its wings and hugs the ball to its chest. It holds the ball for a while and then flies away. Jiangyuan then hears an infant crying on the ice. She rushes there and sees the flesh ball has burst open and inside is a baby boy. The boy pulls a bow with an arrow on it, and aims at the sky. Jiangyuan is delighted to see the baby and carries him in her arms to take him home. Since he was once thrown away, she

Houji from *Drawing Classics Made by Imperial Order* by
Sun Jianai of the Qing Dynasty, depicting how Jiangyuan
abandons Houji in the legend.

names the baby Qi (meaning giving up). Qi liked farming even
as a child and when he grows up he teaches others how to grow
crops. This makes his tribe grow. He is respected as Houji (God
of Agriculture) by his people. His offspring later establish the
Zhou Dynasty.

Qingdu is the daughter of Chenfengshi. She does not marry
until she is twenty (in ancient China women were usually
married at sixteen). One day, she goes to appreciate the scenery
in Sanhe. Suddenly, as a blast of cold wind blows, a dragon
arrives, and impregnates her. She gives birth to a boy baby,
who grows up to be Emperor Yao. The dragon is another form
of Diku and Qingdu is thus another wife of his.

Changyi gives birth to Zhi, who is the successor of Diku.

Diku is buried in Huangxian County, Anyang City in Henan Province, to the west of the resting place of Zhuanxu.

II. The Conflict between Ebo and Shichen

Ebo and Shichen are the first and second sons of Diku. However, the two brothers do not get along. As their differences grow, they start to fight one another in the wild fields with weapons.

Diku fails to reconcile his two sons and has to send them to different places to prevent further conflict. He sends Ebo to Shangqiu in the east to take charge of the bright Shang Star in the eastern sky, and Shichen to Daxia in the west to take charge of the Shen Star in the western sky. Though both stars are in orbit they never meet each other; when the Shang Star appears the Shen Star falls, and vice versa.

The Chinese greatly value a harmonious family and love between brothers. Ebo and Shichen, therefore, set a negative example. Even today, if a conflict occurs between brothers, people refer to it as "brother Shen-Shang."

III. Ebo Steals Fire

Although Ebo used to fight Shichen, he begins his mission in Shangqiu conscientiously.

When he finds that the people who worship the Shang Star do not have fire, he decides to steal fire from heaven. But since the flame is burning and moving all the time, he cannot control and hide it, and is not able to bring it to Shangqiu.

Ebo Platform in Shanqiu City, Henan, built to commemorate Ebo.

Returning to Shangqiu, Ebo thinks hard and finally has an idea. This time, when he goes to heaven, he goes to the celestial fire and burns a thick grass string that he brings with him. Then he blows out the flame, keeping the sparks inside the grass string, and brings it back to Earth quietly. Since then, humans have been able to eat cooked food and use torches.

Soon, the God of Heaven discovers that Ebo has stolen fire. To get the fire back, he unleashes a heavy flood on Earth. The flood swallows farmlands and villages. Since humans have no idea what is happening, many are not able to escape and die. Ebo lets the survivors run away from the calamity and stands alone on the high platform, to guard the last bit of the fire.

A sculpture of Ebo on the Ebo Platform in Shangqiu City, Henan.

After the flood recedes, people come back to the platform to find that the precious fire is still there, burning, while Ebo has closed his eyes forever. To remember him, locals changed the name of the platform to Ebo Altar. Even now, the Ebo Altar stands in Shangqiu, Henan Province, and this story continues to be passed from generation to generation among the locals.

Fire is often thought to be the most important invention in the history of human civilization. There are different sayings about the origin of fire: that it is the creation of saints, such as Fuxi and Suirenshi, or stolen from gods or monsters. In many mythological tales, fire has come from a celestial palace. For example, in Greek mythology, Prometheus steals fire and the method he uses is similar to that of Ebo's in Chinese myth.

IV. Diku's Daughters

Diku has many children and two of his daughters become famous—one becomes a goddess and the other the first ancestor of a southern nationality.

Diku's older daughter is naive and lovely and leads a light-hearted life. She plays every day and everywhere, but, sadly, she dies at an early age. On her deathbed, she laments her short life and says, "I never had any worries and sadness in my life, what I enjoy most is play, but now I am leaving. Today is the fifteenth day of the first lunar month and I hope that you will come to greet my spirit every year on this day so that I will be able to enjoy a pleasant time after death." She becomes Goddess Zigu after death and can predict whether the upcoming year will be good for raising silkworms. The traditional Chinese jubilee falls on the fifteenth day of the first lunar month. People enjoy watching a variety of lanterns, masked parades, fireworks and other traditional celebratory activities. When they enjoy the festival, they do not forget to worship God Zigu. They invite her to earth to have a pleasant time, and at the same time ask her about raising silkworms in the coming spring.

Diku's younger daughter is very beautiful. At that time, the state is reeling from a war against the State of Quanrong. According to the record of Ganbao of the Jin Dynasty in *In Search of the Supernatural*, Marshall Wu of the State of Quanrong was very brave and fierce in battle. Diku sends troops several times to go on a punitive expedition against him but they all return in

In Search of the Supernatural by the Jin Dynasty historian Gan Bao (? – 336) is the most famous collection of esoteric stories of ancient China, recording many stories about deities and spirits, as well as folk tales.

failure. Then, Wu's troop threatens the safety of the capital. At that critical moment, Diku declares to the whole nation that whoever kills Marshal Wu and brings his head to him, will be granted 10,000 *liang* (1 *liang* equals to 50 grams) of gold, will be conferred with the rank of a noble and can marry the princess. However, people are afraid of Wu and no one answers the call.

Soon after, a dog named Panhu in the palace goes missing. But, no one notices as everyone is focused on the war. A few days later, Panhu suddenly appears at the gate of the imperial palace, holding a bleeding head. The dog runs straight to the seat of Diku. When Diku stares at the head, he realizes it is that of Marshal Wu. He also remembers something about the dog.

Panhu is no ordinary dog. Years ago, an elderly woman in the palace came down with a mysterious disease that caused an ear ache that no one could cure. Finally, a doctor found something strange in her ear and pulled it out. It was a worm about seven centimeters long that looked like a silkworm. As soon as the worm was pulled out, the woman recovered. People thought that the worm was very special, put it in a wine container and covered it. They then heard a dog barking under the plate. Curiously, when they uncovered the plate, they found a colorful dog. The dog was named Panhu.

With the death of Marshal Wu, the troops of Quanrong beat a retreat. The royal declaration says the dog should be rewarded. Diku calls his court officials to discuss the matter. All of them say, "Panhu is just a dog. He cannot marry the princess." Diku does not honor his pledge.

But when the daughter hears about this, she goes to her father and says, "Since you already promised to marry me to whoever kills Wu and brings his head to you, you must keep your word or great disaster will befall the country." Diku agrees to marry her to Panhu.

Panhu takes his wife, the princess, away from the capital city. The princess takes off her beautiful dress, puts on clothes made of coarse cloth and follows Panhu to a mountain in the south. Finally, they enter a deep forest and live in a stone cave.

A distressed Diku sends envoys several times to look for his daughter. But, every time, as soon as they go out of the palace gates, dark clouds gather in the sky and a thunderstorm follows. The mountain is completely covered by mists, clouds and rain making it impossible to locate the princess and Panhu.

Over three years, the princess and Panhu give birth to six sons and six daughters. After the death of Panhu, his offspring marry one another and later generations come into existence. They use bark to weave cloth, dye the cloth with colorful grass seeds and then make clothes. All their clothes are designed with a tail to indicate that they are the descendants of Panhu.

Many years pass before the princess finally goes back to the palace to visit her father. Diku immediately sends envoys to bring the children to the palace. It is a clear day. The envoys get them to the palace smoothly. However, these later generations of Panhu cannot communicate with any one, since no one understands their language. They live in the palace for a while, but long to return to the forest. These people gradually form a tribe living in the mountains and forests in the south. Since their forefather Panhu once saved the country and married the daughter of the emperor, they do not pay any tax to the government.

Till today, this legend about Panhu and the princess endures among the Yao and She nationalities in southern China.

The Panhu legend is basically the same as that recorded in the *In Search of the Supernatural*. This version says that the empress of King Gaoxin (also known as Diku) comes down with an earache and a worm is found in her ear. When it is taken out of the ear, it turns into a six-meter long dragon dog and is given the

The Yao people in Guangdong Liannan Yao Nationality Autonomous County make a traditional sacrifice to Panhu during a singing festival.

name Panhu. Later, when an enemy state invades the country, Panhu goes on an expedition and returns successfully. After coming back, he makes a plea for marrying a princess. The first two daughters of the king are not willing to marry Panhu, but the third agrees. But, how can a woman marry a dog? Panhu tells the king that if he is covered under a gold bell for seven day and nights, he will become a man. But while Panhu lies covered under a gold bell, the empress is worried sick. She is afraid that Panhu cannot become human. She cannot hold her anxiety for more than six day and lifts the bell. She sees that the body of Panhu had already changed into a human one; however, the head has not yet changed. As she breaks the rule of waiting for seven days, Panhu's head cannot change.

Thus, Panhu, with human body and dog head, marries the third princess. They have three sons and a daughter. They beg King Gaoxin to grant them surnames. Since the first son was put in a pan (a plate) when he was born, the king grants him the surname of Pan; the second in a lan (a basket), he was named Lan. As the king racks his brains for the third son's surname he hears the sound of thunder and so names him Lei. The young daughter of Panhu marries the warrior Zhong and so her sons and grandsons' surname is Zhong. They make it a rule that the later generations of these four families will marry each other and gradually form a nation; this is the Yao Nationality.

Myths & Legends in the Era of Yao

I. The Birth of Yao

Yao, also known as Fangxun, was the son of Diku and Qingdu and great-grandson of the Yellow Emperor. As described above, Qingdu was impregnated by a divine dragon transformed by Diku and gave birth to Fangxun after being pregnant for fourteen months. Fangxun looked very much like ordinary people, except for his double pupils. His appearance was not handsome, with slanted eyebrows and a head whose upper part was small and lower part large.

His brother Dizhi succeeded the throne upon his father Diku's death. But Dizhi showed little capacity for governing the state and died soon after. So Fangxun ascended the throne and was called Emperor Yao respectfully by the common people. He chose his capital to be Pingyang (now Linfen in Shanxi Province).

II. Miracles during Yao's Rule

Emperor Yao took good care of his subjects and lived a very simple life. All the pillars and girders of his palace were made of unprocessed and unpainted timber. His palace was roofed with couch grass instead of tiles, like the huts of the common people. The steps of the palace were dirt instead of brick and stone. He ate coarse food and drank herb soup. In summer, he wore clothes made of coarse hemp and only added a piece of deerskin in winter to keep out the cold. All his daily utensils were made of clay. He is regarded as the most frugal emperor in legends.

Although he lived such a simple life, Emperor Yao never shirked his responsibilities. When the ordinary people suffered

Emperor Yao.

from hunger, he would blame himself. When they did not have enough to wear, he would again blame himself. When anyone committed a crime, he would blame himself for failing to provide good governance. Emperor Yao kept himself so busy that he had no time to take care of his personal appearance. His two-meter long hair was disheveled and almost touched the ground and he looked emaciated. However, Emperor Yao's distinguished moral character moved his subjects and they were loyal to him.

Emperor Yao touched not only human beings but also impressed the gods. Thus ten natural miracles occurred within one day to declare the confirmation of the God of Heaven of Emperor Yao—horse fodder in the palace turned into rice; auspicious phoenixes dropped on the palace yard from the sky; and calendar grass grew from steps of his palace.

The calendar grass was the sort that could be used as a calendar. The grass grew on the dirt steps of Emperor Yao's palace. On the first day of every month, the grass grew a bean-pod, and another thereafter every day, till the fifteenth day. Starting from the sixteenth, one pod began to drop every day until all had dropped by the end of the month. Then the cycle was renewed. This explains how the grass came to be known as calendar grass.

On the steps of Emperor Yao's palace another peculiar grass, called sycophant grass, also grew. Whenever sycophants passed the steps, the grass would bend with its tips pointing to the evil persons. With the help of this grass, Emperor Yao was able to select a group of talented people with high moral character to hold the posts of ministers to help him govern the state. These virtuous ministers included: Houji in charge of farming; Chui in charge of handcraft production; Gaoyao in charge of the judiciary; Shun in charge of penalty and Qi in charge of military affairs.

With the assistance of these ministers, Emperor Yao made the state prosperous and powerful and people lived a peaceful and wealthy life. In their spare time, people gathered together to play games. One of the games was called "Hitting Rang." People played the game with several wooden strips that were narrow at one end and wide at the other. When playing the game, one strip was put on the ground and everyone attempted to hit the one on the ground from several meters away. The one who hit the strip was the winner.

One day, an old man named Rangfu played the game with other people. He was very skilled in the game and many people came to watch him play. Seeing the scene, one of the spectators said, "It is all because of Emperor Yao's contribution." Hearing this, Rangfu asked him, "What do you mean by saying that? I start work when the sun rises and rest after it sets. I eat what I grow and drink water from the well I have dug. The clothes I wear are made of the cloth I weave. May I ask what help Emperor Yao has given me?" The spectator was rendered speechless.

But the response of Rangfu was what Emperor Yao expected. He never regarded the prosperity and peace in his country as his accomplishment. He considered it to be his duty as an emperor and did not expect the people to show gratitude for the happiness they enjoyed. The era of Emperor Yao was one of freedom and Rangfu had a free mind.

III. Miracle Judge Gaoyao

Gaoyao was a judge appointed by Emperor Yao. Gaoyao had an expressionless face, greenish melon-like skin and a bird's beak, and was resolute and decisive in speech.

Xiezhi, auspicious one-horned divine best of legend, represents justice.

Gaoyao was capable and experienced, and also impartial and incorruptible. No matter how difficult a situation was, he could handle it. To a great extent, Gaoyao relied a one-horned divine goat (Xiezhi) he raised. The goat had cyan-colored hairs all over its body and one horn on its head. It was tame, faithful, upright and capable of distinguishing between right and wrong. When two people were at odds and no one could judge the dispute, the goat would gore the one who was in the wrong. Gaoyao always brought his goat to hear cases. When he was unable to make judgment, the goat could help him. It would gore the criminal but not the innocent person. Looking at its reaction, Gaoyao could know whether the defendant was guilty or not.

Because of Gaoyao, the legal system in Emperor Yao's era was fair and there was never a wrongly judged case.

IV. Ten Suns in the Sky and the Severe Drought

Although Emperor Yao did his utmost to govern the country well, he suffered many calamities in his life. One such crisis was that ten suns once appeared simultaneously in the sky and caused a severe drought.

The ten suns born to Dijun and Xihe lived in a large mulberry tree in the east of the Earth. Every day, one sun used to patrol the sky on a three-claw crow while the other nine rested in the tree. For a long time, they took turns to patrol the sky, but something went wrong during the reign of Emperor Yao. The ten suns left the tree at the same time and wandered around in the sky all at once. Plants and crops were scorched, the rivers dried out, the earth cracked and even rocks were almost melted down.

An unprecedented drought made human beings eat everything that could be eaten and farming suffered. As they became

Three-claw crow in a Han Dyansty stone carving.

exhausted, they were no longer able to save themselves from attacks by beasts. Giant boars, long vipers, as well as Yayu, Zaochi, Jiuying and other wild beasts and monsters came out their dens and began to kill human beings at will.

The helpless people turned to Nüchou, a sorceress, to pray for rain. Nüchou had great supernatural powers and often rode on a one-horn dragon-fish wandering around the world. The dragon-fish had four legs and a huge body that could swallow a whole ship. When swimming in the sea, it often created waves. It could live on land and also fly. Escorted by large crowds, Nüchou arrived on the mountaintop to pray for rain. She lay down with her face toward the sky to pray to the God of Heaven for rain. But this time, her supernatural powers failed. The burning sunshine of the ten suns shone on her face relentlessly. Unable to withstand the heat, Nüchou covered her face with her wide sleeve but could not block the sunshine. She was scorched to death on the mountaintop.

V. Yi Shot Suns

At this time there was a deity, Yi, in heaven who was very good at archery. Any bird flying past him would drop down just at the sound made by Yi's bow as he shot an arrow. The God of Heaven sent Yi to the world of men to teach the ten suns a lesson and save mankind. Before his departure, God gave him a big red bow and a bag of white arrows. The Chinese classic the *Huainanzi* says that Yi was the archer sent by Emperor Yao to shoot the suns.

Yi arrived in the world of men and saw the ten suns still riding on the three-clawed crows and wandering around in the sky. Yi took

Yi Shooting Suns, Liang Qide.

Yi Shooting Suns, carved on a piece of Qing architecture, discovered in Shiyan, Hubei Province.

down the big red bow from his shoulder, fitted the white arrow to the string and aimed it at one sun. A ray of white light flashed by and the arrow hit the chest of the crow. The bow and arrow given by God was indeed extremely powerful. The arrow penetrated the crow's chest and it died instantly. Its black feathers came whirling down from the sky. Having lost the three-clawed crow, the sun fell down into the East Sea. Yi shot eight other arrows in one shot and eight suns fell into the East Sea. The embers of the falling suns and the black feathers of the three-clawed crows were all over the sky. The last sun obeyed Yi's order tamely and returned to its original orbit.

The nine dead suns fell into the East Sea and turned into an enormous stone called Jiaowo, 30,000 *li* wide and 40,000 *li* long. Jiaowo was extremely hot and converted the surrounding seawater into white steam that disappeared into the thin air. If there were not thousands of rivers flowing into it, the East Sea would have dried up.

The sky became serene again, the Earth cooled and the severe drought ended. Yi began to fight the monsters that had brought destruction.

In the southern marsh there was a monster called Zaochi. It looked like a human being, but with teeth more than one meter long, like chisels. It fought Yi with a long spear, but was defeated. It fled to the East of the Kunlun Mountain, but was shot dead by Yi with one arrow.

Yi then went to the riverbank of Xiongshui River in the North, where there was a nine-headed snake named Jiuying. It could spout both water and fire. Although it was fearsome, it was no match for Yi and was shot dead in the river.

In the east marsh, a giant bird caused havoc by triggering a gale with its huge wings, destroying houses built by man. Yi was afraid that he would not be able to kill it with one arrow. So he tied a solid rope to the end of the arrow. When the bird flew by, Yi shot

Yayu, a legendary man-eating monster, from *Shan Hai Jing: the Northern Mountain*, Jiang Yinghao, Ming Dynasty.

it and hit the target. He held the rope to pull the wounded bird to him and killed it.

The huge evil snake that lived in Dongting Lake was chopped into several pieces by Yi, and the monster Yayu in the Ruoshui River by the Kunlun Mountain in the West was also killed by Yi. The myth mentioned in Chapter 6 says that Yayu was a deity who guarded the Yellow Emperor in the Ruoshui River to show his gratitude to the Yellow Emperor for bringing him back to life. Its status was different from the one in Yi's story.

Finally, Yi arrived in the mulberry woods that used to be sacred but were now occupied by a giant boar. Yi caught the boar, killed it and cooked it to sanctify it for the God of Heaven. However, the God and his wife were not happy, perhaps because Yi shot the nine suns dead and broke the original order of the universe. Despite his outstanding efforts, God abrogated Yi's divine status and refused him to return to heaven. Since then, Yi has had to live in the world of men.

The Chinese myth of the ten suns has some similarities to the Greek myth of Phaeton. Phaeton, son of Eos and Celphlus, asked his father to allow him to drive the Chariot of the Sun for a day. But he was unable to control it and it began to run towards Earth. Because of its scorching heat, rivers on Earth dried up, forests caught fire and people were plunged into an abyss of misery. Zeus had to stop him with a thunderbolt. Phaeton fell into the River Eridanus and drowned.

VI. Yi and Luoshen's Love Affairs

Yi felt resentful at being deprived of his celestial status but his tragedy did not end with having to roam the world of men.

His wife Chang'e used to be an immortal in heaven but now came to the world of men with Yi. But Yi often wandered outside,

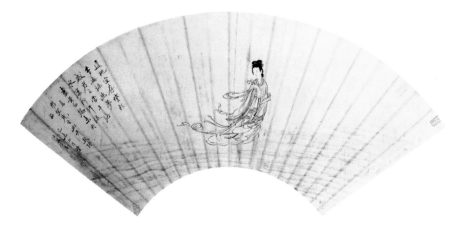

Luoshen depicted on an ancient Chinese fan.

leaving Chang'e alone at home. Chang'e felt very lonely and the couple's relationship began to suffer.

One day, Yi goes hunting with his bow and arrows. He arrives at the banks of the Luohe River. The water flows gently and the wide bank is covered in luxuriant woods and beautiful flowers. A pretty goddess and some fairies are amusing themselves here. Yi is attracted by the goddess and one night he dreams of being with her.

The goddess is called Luopin or Luoshen. It turns out she is the daughter of Fuxi, the God of the East Heaven. Unfortunately, she drowns in the Luohe River and is made the Goddess Luohe. The Luohe River was a branch of the Yellow River. Goddess Luohe was also the wife of Hebo, the God of the Yellow River. Hebo used to be a human being called Bingyi. He drowned when crossing the Yellow River and is assigned to be the god of rivers. Hebo, being dissolute by nature, often took a group of fairies to amuse himself. Luoshen therefore became depressed. Just as Yi was attracted by Luoshen's beauty, Luoshen fell in love with Yi. When they met again, they both fell into the river of love and united.

Detail from *Ode to Lushen*, a Song Dynasty copy of Gu Kaizhi's original of the Eastern Jin Dynasty (c.345–406), Palace Museum, Beijing. The picture depicts the meeting between Luoshen and Cao Zhi.

Hebo had numerous underlings, with turtles as his attendants and a cuttlefish as his secretary. They kept Hebo informed of everything. Yi and Luoshen's love affair could not be kept secret. On finding out about his wife's affairs with Yi, Hebo burned with anger. But he knew he was not Yi's equal. If he had a duel with Yi, he would surely be defeated. So, he turned into a white dragon and spied on Yi near the riverbank. Yi saw that the white dragon harbored malicious thoughts and shot an arrow at him, piercing Hebo's left eye.

In hatred and fear, Hebo complained to God, pointing to his eye. God asks, "Why did Yi shoot at you?" Hebo replies, "I turned into a white dragon and swam in the river." God said, "If you had guarded your divine place in earnest, how could Yi hurt you? A dragon is a lowly animal and that is why you got shot at. What crime has Yi commited?" Hebo returned to the Yellow River angrily because he was blind in one eye and had also been spurned by God.

VII. The Legend of Hebo's Wedding

Hebo returned to the world of men and indulged his lust since he could not stop Luoshen and Yi's relationship. He threatened human beings by making the Zhanghe River flood the lands of the villagers if they did would not send him a beautiful woman as his wife. The frightened locals would choose a beautiful young woman, dress her up and send her to Hebo by putting her on the bed of flowers that would float on the river. The bed would sink after a while and the woman would be carried off by Hebo.

Finding a wife for Hebo then became a custom, which continued till the Warring States Period (475–221 B.C.). The sorcerers and sorceresses along the Zhang River took the opportunity to make money by finding a wife for Hebo every year. Once, Ximenbao, the county magistrate, was present at one such wedding. He said, "The woman is not beautiful enough. The sorceresses should go find Hebo and tell him that a more beautiful bride will be chosen for him." Then he threw the sorceresses into the river. The sorceresses did not return. Ximenbao then said, "They did not handle this well. Other sorcerers should go down the river to press them." All the sorcerers knelt down begging for mercy. Ximenbao thus eradicated the abuse of finding wives for Hebo. To prevent Hebo's revenge, he also told the people to dig twelve ditches to avoid the danger of flooding once and for all.

VIII. Chang'e Flying to the Moon

The love affair with Luoshen could not dispel Yi's pain, for he finally had to face death after he lost his immortal, divine status. He began to seek the pill of immortality. He knew the

Chang'e Flying to the Moon,
Ren Shuaiying.

Queen Mother of the West held the pill and she lived on Kunlun Mountain. By his courage and immense power, he passed the flaming hill and Ruoshui River, climbed to the top of Kunlun Mountain and met the Western Mother Goddess, who was the goddess in charge of plague and punishment. She looked very ominous, with a human-like body, tiger teeth and a leopard's tail. But she had a kind heart. When she heard Yi's story, she felt sorry for him and gave him the pill of immortality. Yi was overjoyed. He hid the pill after returning home and decided to choose an appropriate day to take it.

Then an unexpected thing happened. Deeply hurt by Yi and Luoshen's love affairs, Chang'e wanted to leave her husband Yi.

Chang'e, painted by Xiao Huizhu, depicting the lonely life of Chang'e on the moon.

One day, she asked the sorcerer Youhuang to make a prediction for her future. Youhuang conducted a ritual with grass and told her, "One graceful woman will go to the remote west alone. On her way there will be darkness. But she will surely reach her destination as long as she is not afraid. She will have a bright future and many offspring." Youhuang's prediction helped Chang'e make up her mind. She returned home to find the pill of immortality and swallowed it. Instantly, she flew to the moon.

Soon after Chang'e entered the moon, her body began to change: her eyes popped out, her neck and shoulders shrunk together, her belly swelled up, and her white smooth skin turned yellowish brown and grew many pimples. She wanted to cry, but could only let out a croak. She wanted to run away, but could only grovel on the ground, crawling step by step. In an instant, the beautiful Chang'e was turned into an ugly toad. With her on the desolate moon, there is only one cassia tree and a white rabbit constantly pounding the elixir of immortality.

Did Youhuang cheat Chang'e? Chang'e landed on the moon, so her future was bright. The toad can produce numerous eggs at once, so she certainly had many offspring. But perhaps, it was God's punishment for her attempt to live forever in violation of his will.

This story has other variations. The most popular is that Chang'e becomes the beautiful goddess of moon, but is lonely with only the rabbit for company.

After losing his wife and the pill of immortality, Yi becomes desperate. He takes on several apprentices to teach them archery. The most outstanding of these is Pangmeng, who can defeat anyone except his master Yi. In order to become the number one archer in the world, Pangmeng finds a way to kill the great hero by battering Yi with a peach wood stick. This marks the end of Yi's tragic life.

IX. Gun Tamed the Raging Waters

According to legend, Emperor Yao sat on the throne for seventy years. Therefore, he faced more disasters than other emperors. After the drought passed, a deluge follows, caused by Gonggong, God of Water. After he is defeated by Zhuanxu, Gonggong flees for his life and hides in a deep pool. In the era of Emperor Yao, he emerges and makes all rivers flow backwards, leading to the deluge.

Emperor Yao calls all his ministers to choose the right person to tame the flood. The ministers recommend Gun. Emperor Yao is

Bronze statue by Jiang Haiyan in the form of a dragon, depicting the birth of Dayu from the belly of Gun, Dayu Myth Garden on the banks of the Hanjiang, Wuhan.

not sure that Gun can fulfill the task because he feels Gun is too self-willed. But eventually Yao lets Gun try.

Gun is the grandson of the Yellow Emperor (Huangdi). After receiving Emperor Yao's order, he asks the sorcerer Daming to make a prediction for him. Daming says, "It is a very inauspicious thing having a beginning but no ending." Although the result of the divination is not good, Gun accepts the task and sets off to tame the floods. He leads the people to build dams but they are of no use. For nine years, he tries to control the floods but all his efforts are to no avail.

As Gun knits his brows in worry, an owl and a tortoise devise a plan: "There is a special soil called Xirang (rest soil) in the heaven. It can grow automatically. You need only to get a small piece and throw it into the water. The Xirang will grow bigger and bigger and become high mountains. You will succeed in stopping the floods with it." Gun is delighted to hear this. He goes to heaven and steals a piece of Xirang.

He throws the special soil into the surging flood and sees a piece of land growing at the place the Xirang was dropped. It grows bigger and higher and blocks the floodwaters, forcing back the rivers. The floodwaters recede and people who have fled return to their homes.

The God of Heaven flies into a rage when he finds out that Xirang was stolen. He sends Zhu Rong, the God of Fire, to the world of men to arrest Gun and put him to death at Yushan. The God of Heaven takes back Xirang and the floods make a comeback and inundate the lands once more. This lasts until the era of Emperor Shun. Sorcerer Daming's prophesy comes true.

Gun's corpse does not rot after his death. The God of Heaven becomes fearful that Gun may revive and sends people to cut his belly. When they do this, a dragon emerges from his belly and rises to the sky. This dragon is Gun's son, Yu. Gun's corpse finally turns into a three-legged turtle and disappears under the Yushan Mountain.

X. Emperor Yao's Demise

Emperor Yao believed that the emperor's throne should belong to a wise and capable person. He thinks his son Danyu is not up to the task and appoints Shun, known for his high morals and brilliance, to the throne. Such a system played a special role in China's history.

Emperor Yao was worshiped widely after his death and people built many tombs and mausoleums for him. According to *Shan Hai Jing* and other books, in Yue Mountain, Di Mountain and other places, there are tombs and mausoleums of Emperor Yao. There are many temples commemorating Yao, the most famous being the Yao Temple in Linfen, Shanxi Province. To the present day, people hold many ceremonies to commemorate this sage emperor of prehistoric times.

Myths & Legends in the Era of Shun

I. Birth of Shun and His Youth

Legend has it that Emperor Shun was the eighth generation of the Yellow Emperor's offspring. His father was Gusou, meaning blind old man. It was not his original name and he was called by the name only after he became blind. His mother was Wodeng.

Gusou and Wodeng lived in Yaoxu (now Juanxian County in Shandong Province). One day, the sun shone brightly after the rains and a beautiful rainbow appeared in the sky. Wodeng was attracted by the rainbow and looked at it for a long time. She did not know that the rainbow meant that heaven and earth were mating. Thus she became pregnant without knowing it. The night before the baby is born, Wodeng dreams that a phoenix descends in front of her claiming it is her son. Gusou consults the book *Dreams of the Yellow Emperor* and finds that according to the book, such a dream promises that among his offspring there will be one with exalted status.

When Shun is born, each of his bright eyes has two pupils, like Emperor Yao.

But soon Shun's mother dies and Gusou becomes blind. The young Shun begins to take care of his father. Later, Gusou remarries and with his second wife, he has a son called Xiang and a daughter called Keshou. Gusou thinks Shun is the phoenix of his dream, but a series of misfortunes makes him dislike Shun. Instead, he takes a liking to his younger son Xiang. Shun's stepmother and Xiang treat Shun terribly. However, Shun show filial piety to both his father and stepmother and endures his parents' abuse silently. He also tries to take care of his badly behaved stepbrother. His stepmother speaks ill of him to Gusou many times and finally they decided to murder him.

One day, they tell Shun the water in the well of their house is not clear and needs to be cleaned. Shun takes some tools gets down into the well. He cleans the well and suddenly finds himself in total darkness. It turns out that Gusou and his stepmother have blocked the mouth of the well, in an attempt to kill him. Shun is deeply anguished but can do nothing but wait to die. However, his filial piety touches the God of Heaven and a miracle occurs: a channel which leads to his neighbor's well, appears out of nowhere. Shun is saved, but he knows he cannot return home, because his father and stepmother will try other ways to kill him. He does not want them to have the burden of killing their son.

Shun flees to Lishan (now in the southeast of Yongji County in Shanxi Province) and lives there by farming. Because of his good character, people liked to be his neighbors. One year later, the place where he lives becomes a village, a town two years later and a big city three years later. Influenced by him, people in the neighborhood all become kind and modest.

Around that time, Emperor Yao is looking for a sage. In order to test his character and ability, he gives his daughters Ehuang and Nüying to Shun in marriage. After Shun gets married, he misses his parents even more and leaves Lishan for home with his two wives.

The family is united. Shun and his two wives show respect to the parents, but it is difficult to change the nature of Gusou, his stepmother and stepbrother Xiang, who still want to harm him.

One day, Gusou asks Shun to clean the barn roof. Shun agrees and tells his two wives to help him. Ehuang and Nüying warn him of Gusou's bad intentions. But Shun says, "I must obey my father. But if anything bad happens, his reputation will suffer. How can I obey my father's order but also save his reputation?" Ehuang and Nüying take out a dress with the pattern of a flying bird and ask him to put it on. Shun climbs onto the high roof of the barn to clean. Gusou and Xiang set the barn on fire and the flames soon spread to the roof. Surrounded by the fire, Shun has to jump down from the roof. The dress he wears looks like a flying bird that carries him on its back and brings him to the ground safely.

Gusou and the step-mother and step-brother make several attempts to kill Shun, but with Ehuang and Nüying's help, he escapes every time. Yet, Shun never complains and always treats his father, stepmother and stepbrother with kindness and respect.

II. Shun Ascends to the Throne

After his test of Shun, Emperor Yao is convinced that Shun is a filial son. He then appoints Shun to deal with government affairs and finally orders Shun to pass through a forest. When he enters the forest, Shun finds himself in rain and wind, with thunder and lightning. But he is not afraid and advances bravely. Even the fierce tigers and leopards, voracious jackals and poisonous vipers on the way dare not offend him. Shun safely cut through the forest

Emperor Shun.

and comes back to Emperor Yao, who abdicates and hands the throne to Shun.

After ascending the throne, Shun returns home with his attendants to visit his parents. Despite being the emperor, Shun continues to show respect to his parents. Gusou finally realizes that Shun is the phoenix he once dreamed of and is touched by Shun's act of disregarding his maltreatment. His bitterness toward Shun vanishes and father and son become reconciled.

Emperor Shun makes his brother Xiang the duke of Youbi Kingdom. Xiang too is touched and gives up his evil ways.

III. Buried at the Jiuyi Mountain

The great flood in Emperor Yao's rule does not subside as Gun fails to tame it. After ascending the throne, Emperor Shun appoints Gun's son Dayu (the Great Yu) to continue taming the flood, and it is he who finally succeeds in controlling the waters. In his old age, Emperor Shun abdicates the throne in favor of Dayu, who has both ability and integrity.

Emperor Shun enjoys a peaceful life and tours around the country. When he arrives at Cangwu (now Ningyuan County, Hunan Province), he falls ill and dies. Hearing the sad news of their husband's death, Ehuang and Nüying begin to cry and

Ehuang and Nuying, painted by Qing Dynasty artist Wu Youru (1894).

Traditional Chinese New Year picture, *Twenty-Four Filial Sons.*

wherever their tears fall, emerald green bamboos with flecks spring up; these are the mottled bamboos of today.

Shun was buried near Jiuyi Mountain after his death. It is said that there were many monsters guarding the grave. Among them, Weiwei, a fearsome two-headed snake, was the most well-known. Many people died just looking at him, similar to those who looked at the viper-haired Medusa in Greek mythology.

Emperor Shun is a moral role model in China. The *Twenty-Four Filial Sons*, a book that records famous filial sons in ancient China, ranks Emperor Shun as the first. His stories are popular among the people. There is a place called Lishan Mountain in Shanxi, Shandong, Henan, Hebei and other places and local people regard the Lishan in their locality as the place where Emperor Shun farmed. In Hongtong County, Shanxi Province, there is a temple for Emperor Shun and every year a sacrificial event is held there.

The Twenty-Four Filial Sons, compiled by Guo Jujing of the Yuan Dynasty (1206–1368) contains twenty-four well-known ancient stories about dutiful sons.

Myths & Legends in the Era of Dayu

I. The Birth of Dayu

There are two versions of the story on the birth of Dayu. The first one is that he was a dragon that emerged out of Gun's belly. The second version is that Gun's wife Youshen, who lived in Wenchuan (now Wenchuan County in Sichuan), got pregnant after she swallowed a pearl. Later, when she went to the riverbank, her chest suddenly burst and she gave birth to Dayu. Blood spattered on the white stones on the riverbank and till today the stones there have red spots.

II. Orders to Control the Floodwater

Emperor Shun ordered Yu to succeed his father to control the floods and the God of Heaven gave him the magic soil of Xirang to help him to control the floodwaters.

In order to defeat Gonggong, the god of water, and put an end to flooding, Dayu held a meeting of all deities at Maoshan to discuss what should be done. Since Maoshan was the place where the deities gathered together to discuss plans, it was also called Huijishan.

All deities arrived at Huiji Mountain on time to discuss how to control the flood, except for Fangfeng. Fangfeng was more than ten meters tall, with a dragon's head, ox's ears and a single eye and eyebrow. His arrogance irritated Dayu, who gave orders to execute him at once. Because of his tall stature, the executioner could not reach his head. A tall stand was therefore built and the executioner

Xiangliu, the nine-headed snake from *Shang Hai Jing: Overseas Northern*, Wang Fu, Qing Dynasty.

Bronze statue *Fighting with Xiangliu*, located in the Dayu Myth Garden on the Hanjiang Bank in Wuhan, which was created by Jiang Haiyan.

stood on it to chop down Fangfeng's head. Seeing Fangfeng being executed, all other deities shuddered with fear and dared not violate Dayu's orders.

Dayu first led the deities to expel Gonggong so as to remove the cause of the flood. Then they killed Gonggong's subordinate, the nine-headed snake Xiangliu. Xiangliu's blood stank and no grasses would grow where it spilled. Dayu had to fetch soil from elsewhere to cover the soil stained with Xiangliu's blood. But soon after, the ground sank. Dayu then dug a big pool there and built a stage by the pool to hold a memorial ceremony for the God of Heaven to suppress Xiangliu. Another Gonggong subordinate Fuyou fled to the bottom of the Huai River and turned into a red bear. The bear always smiles, but everyone who meets it suffers misfortunes. If it appeared outside the main room of a house, all the people of the county would be scared and if it entered the room, the ruler would die. When Dayu flung Xirang into the floodwaters, land appeared instantly and in some places there were even high mountains. But the watercourse on the land remains blocked. Dayu changed his way of thinking and began to dig channels to conduct water to the sea. He first handles the Yellow River in the North.

The Yellow River, traversing the land of the Central Plain, was the biggest and most important for the Chinese since ancient times. Legend has it that the Yellow River originated in the northeast of the sacred Kunlun Mountain. After flowing

Fresco depicting Dayu's efforts to control the floods, Daotong Temple of the Songyang Academy in Dengfeng, Henan.

out of Kunlun Mountain, it was blocked by Jishi Mountain. Dayu cut a huge hole at the foot of the mountain and made the water of the Yellow River pass through Jishi Mountain smoothly. The hole was later called Shimen. River water gushed from Shimen, passed a stretch of fields and arrived at Longmen Mountain. In ancient times, Longmen Mountain linked with Luliang Mountain, blocking the watercourse of the Yellow River and forming an ocean. Dayu used his magic powers to cut the Longmen Mountain to make way for the water. The torrential water flowed down vigorously after passing Longmen Mountain. The mountain now looked like two huge gates, so Dayu named it Longmen Mountain. It is said that carps in the rivers and lakes would swim against the current along the Yellow River to Longmen Mountain. Those that could pass through this section of water would become dragons and those that failed would remain as carps. The water to the Yellow River dashed out of Longmen Mountain, entered Henan Province and was blocked by Dizhu Mountain. Dayu cut three gaps in the mountain in one breath to form Shenmen, Guimen and Renmen (meaning gate for deities, gate for ghost and gate for human beings respectively), which were called Sanmen (three gates), now Sanmenxia. Since then, the Yellow River has cut across the north China plain and rushed to the East Sea.

After he controlled the Yellow River, Dayu went to other places to handle the rest of the rivers.

III. Dayu's Tragic Marriage

With his focus on controlling the rivers, Dayu soon reached the age of thirty. He prayed to the God of Heaven for revelation of his intended marriage. A white fox with nine tails appeared on the field. Dayu thought carefully and realized the meaning of the fox: "white means I'm a common person; while the nine tails foretell that I will become emperor in the future." A ballad that circulated at that time in Tushan went: "The white nine-tail fox is running on the field. Who comes to my house to be the guest, he will become the emperor. If he marries into my family, the family will prosper." So Dayu went to Tushan and married Nüjiao, daughter of Tushanshi. Just four days after his marriage, he left home to resume his work taming the floodwaters.

The steep Huanyuan Mountain (now in Yanshi County, Henan Province) blocked the watercourse and Dayu chiseled the mountain everyday. His wife Nüjiao lived in the Middle High Mountains, Songshan (now Dengfeng County in Henan Province), and sent food to Dayu everyday. Because the stone of the Huanyuan Mountain was too hard to chisel, Dayu had to turn into a bear to dig the mountain. To prevent his wife from seeing him as a bear, Dayu set a drum at the foot of the mountain and told Nüjiao to send the food only when she heard the sound of the drum. Nüjiao agreed.

One day, when Dayu was chiseling the mountain, a stone fell down and hit the drum. But Dayu did not notice and continued his work. Hearing the sound of the drum, Nüjiao went to send food for her husband and saw the bear digging at the top of the mountain. She knew it was her husband. She felt very ashamed and ran away. Dayu saw his wife and ran after her. Nüjiao could not run fast because she was pregnant. She had almost been caught by her husband when she ran to the south slope of Songshan Mountain, so she turned into a giant stone.

Qimushi (northern side), located by the foot of Songshan, Dengfeng in Henan Province. Legend has it that this is where Dayu's wife gave birth to her son Qi.

Qimushi (southern side)

Dayu was devastated. He said to the stone, "Please leave the son to me." Before he finished his words, the back of the stone split and a boy fell out crying. Because the son was born from the split stone, he was named Qi, meaning split, and the stone was called Qimushi, literally stone of Qi's mother.

IV. Having all the Rivers under Control

The Huai River, another of China's big rivers, originated in Tongbai Mountain in Henan Province. The God of Huai River was called Wuzhiqi and was extremely ferocious, often causing floods. Dayu went there three times, but he was unable to cut a watercourse because of strong winds and heavy rain. He knew there must be a divine being behind the trouble. So he called all

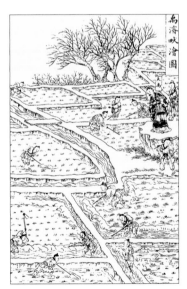

deities to inquire about the matter. With the deities' help, he caught Wuzhiqi. The God of Huai River looked like a giant monkey, with a neck more than ten meters long, a high forehead, a flat nose and a pair of golden, shining eyes. Although he was caught, he continued to struggle to run free. Dayu had to fasten an iron chain to his neck, pierce his nose with a golden bell and imprison him under Gu Mountain. Later, Dayu cut Huai River and made the river water flow smoothly to the sea.

Dayu left his footprints all over the country and succeeded in controlling all the rivers. But there were cuts and bruises all over his body and he changed beyond recognition.

Woodcut of Yu, depicting the scene of Dayu directing irrigation work.

He became emaciated, with sunken cheeks and a mouth like a bird's beak. He could scarcely move his limbs. No nails were left on his hands and all the hair on his legs had fallen off.

Peace reigned over the land. Dayu designated deities to measure the land and got the following results: the length from east to west was 200,033500 *lis* and 75 steps (equals to 100,017,750 kilometers and 125 meters) and measured the same from north to south.

After accomplishing this task, Dayu crossed Ruoshui River on a cart and climbed the sacred Zhong Mountain,

Picture depicting Emperor Yao giving Dayu awards because of his success in controlling the floods, from a Ming Dynasty woodcut.

where the Yellow Emperor grew white jade and deities had gatherings. He offered sacrifices to the God of Heaven and later succeeded the throne, after Emperor Shun. His mausoleum is in Huijishan in Shaoxing, Zhejiang Province, and there are still sacrifices offered to him there every year.

Other Myths & Legends

I. Kuafu Chasing the Sun

According to the *Shan Hai Jing*, the sun moving around in the sky every day aroused a giant's attention. He was Kuafu, the eighth generation offspring of Emperor Yan and grandson of Houtu. He lived on a mountain called Chengdu Zaitian in the wildness of the North. He liked to play with snakes and had yellow snakes on each of his ears and both his hands. Kuafu was tall, sturdy and nimble. He ran like a flying bird and nobody could catch him. After noticing the sun's fast movement in the sky, he decided to chase the sun to compete with it.

Riding on the three-clawed bird, the sun flashed across the sky and flew to remote Yugu in the west. Kuafu chased after it with long strides. When the sun slowly set in Yugu at dusk, Kuafu arrived. Kuafu was excited and proud of his success. In order to have a good look at his rival, he entered the sun.

Kuafu Chasing the Sun, from *Shan Hai Jing: Overseas Northern*, painted by Jiang Yinghao, Ming Dynasty.

Kuanfu did not know that the sun was like a burning furnace. Unable to bear the extreme heat, he left the sun and ran toward the Yellow River. Arriving at this there, he drank desperately. But as his body was indeed enormous, Kuafu drank all the river water. Even this was not enough for him and he had to run to Wei River, a branch of the Yellow River. It, too, was soon drained by Kuafu. Still feeling thirsty, he then ran to the Great Lake in the North. With a circumference of over thousands of *lis*, the Great Lake was huge and all the fowls in the world went there to multiply their offspring and to change their feathers. Kuafu wanted to find enough water to quench his terrible thirst but the Great Lake was too far away, and he was exhausted. He died in the wild Northwest before he could reach the lake and his walking stick turned into a huge, lush peach forest.

The offspring of Kuafu founded a country called Bofu or Kuafu at the west of the peach forest. They inherited Kuafu's tall stature

Kuafu holding a green snake in his right hand and a yellow one in his left, *Shan Hai Jing: Overseas Northern*, painted by Jiang Yinghao, Ming Dynasty.

and fondness for snakes. Everyone held a green snake in his right hand and a yellow one in his left.

Later, Bofu vanished but the peach forest remained and was called Peach Village. Near this village is Kuafu Mountain. According to local history, it is now in Linbao County in the west of Henan Province. Traditionally, some local people believe they are offspring of Kuafu.

II. Yugong Moving Mountains

The text *Liezi*, states that a ninety-year old man called Yugong, meaning foolish man, once lived on Bei Mountain. There were two other large mountains, Taihang and Wangwu, in front of his house, which caused his family great inconvenience. So he gathered his family and said, "The two mountains have given us too much trouble, let's move them." His children and grandchildren all agreed.

The family got to work the very next day. The weaker members dug the soil and those stronger hammered the stones to open the mountain. They collected the soil and stones in baskets and carried them to Bohai Sea. It took them more than half a year make this journey. But the brave family continued undaunted. They were soon joined by their neighbors. Even the young son of a widow, who just lost his milk teeth, pitched in to help. The work went on in full swing.

At the turning of the Yellow River, there lived an old man called Zhisou, meaning wise man. Upon seeing the family attempting to move the mountains, he said to Yugong: "You are

Yuging Moving Mountains, Xu Beihong.

so foolish. With one foot already in the grave, you will be able to do nothing to the Taihang and Wangwu mountains. Why are you doing such a useless thing?"

Yugong replied: "You are wrong. Your insight is not as good as that of my neighboring widow and child. Even if I am dead, I have children, and when my children are dead, there are still my grandchildren. My family will keep growing. Although Taihang and Wangwu mountains are tall, they will not grow taller. If we are determined, we can surely move the two mountains!" His reply left Zhisou speechless.

Hearing Yugong's words, a deity feared that Yugong's continued digging would ruin the home of the God of Mountains. So he immediately reported the matter to the God of Heaven. He was moved by their determination and sent two giants, sons of Kua'eshi, to take the two mountains away, placing one east of Suzhou and the other south of Yongzhou.

III. Cow herd and Vega

In ancient times, there were two brothers who broke up their family and lived apart. The older brother got the fertile lands and house while the younger one only got a cow, with whom he became very close.

One day, the cow told him that on the seventh day of the seventh lunar month, fairies would arrive in the world of men. If he could take one fairy's skirt away, he could marry her. In the evening, the cow herd went to the lake and hid himself in the brushwood. Soon the gates of the palace in the heaven opened and seven fairies flew to the lake. They removed their skirts, jumped into the lake and began to wash. Cowboy took one skirt and hid it. After the bath, the fairies put on their skirts and flew back to heaven, but the youngest fairy could not find her skirt and was unable to fly away. She found the cow herd with her skirt and married him. It turned out that she was Vega, the seventh daughter of the God of Heaven, in charge of creating beautiful clouds for the sky. Vega used her magic powers to create a fully-equipped house and lived happily with the cow herd. They loved each other very much and later, Vega bore two babies—a boy and a girl.

Unfortunately, the God of Heaven and his wife, Western Mother Goddess, burst out in anger upon hearing that Vega had married a cow herd. They sent divine troops to capture Vega and take her back to heaven. With the help of his cow, the cow herd put his daughter and son into two baskets and carried them

Traditional Chinese New Year picture *Cow Herd and Vega*.

Meeting at the Magpie Bridge, Liang Qide.

to chase after his wife. Seeing that he was about to catch up, Western Mother Goddess took out her gold hairpin and created a huge roaring river to keep him from Vega. The couple looked at one another from opposite sides of the river and cried. They later turned into the stars Altair and Vega in constellations on the two sides of the Milky Way.

On the next seventh day of the seventh lunar month, many magpies flew to the heaven river and made a bridge for the cow herd and his wife to unite. Their undying love made the God of Heaven relent to allow them to meet on the seventh day of the seventh lunar month every year.

Appendix 1
Major Characters in Chinese Myths & Legends

Pangu
God of creation. Became all things on earth after his death.

Nüwa
Goddess of Protection of Humankind and Goddess of Marriage. She created humans with clay and mended the Heaven with colored stones.

Fuxi
The son of the god Leize and ancestor of humankind; the husband of **Nüwa**. In another version, he was the brother of **Nüwa** but married her in order to reproduce. He later became Emperor of the Eastern Heaven, assisted by the God of Wood, **Goumang**, in charge of the East Heaven and spring.

Yandi
Also named **Shennong**, **Yandi** is God of Farming and Medicine. Later, he became Southern God of Heaven, assisted by the God of Fire, **Zhu Rong**, in charge of South Heaven and summer.

Huangdi
The Yellow Emperor. Defeated **Yandi** and **Chiyou** in a series of wars and sought the highest seat as the Central God of Heaven and established order with him at the core. His wife **Leizu** was the first person to raise silkworms.

Shaohao
West God of Heaven and son of **Huangdi**. He is in charge of the West Heaven and autumn, assisted by his son, the God of Gold **Rushou**.

Zhuanxu
North God of Heaven and grandson of **Huangdi**. He is in charge of North Heaven and winter and later becomes the Central God of Heaven, succeeding **Huangdi**.

Dijun
A great god. He produced ten suns with his wife **Xihe** and twelve moons with his wife **Changxi**. When the ten suns appeared at the same time, causing disasters, the hero **Yi** shot nine down.

Western Mother Goddess

Living in Yaochi, abode of immortals in Mount. Kunlun, she is in charge of murrain and penalty. She once met with the hero **Yi,** who shot down the suns, and awarded him with an immortal pill on Mount Kunlun.

Chiyou

The most fearful god in Chinese mythology, with an ox head and human body. He was once the subordinate of **Yandi** after whose failure he became subordinate of **Huangdi.** He later launched a rebellion against Emperor **Huangdi** and was killed.

Gonggong

Son of the God of Fire **Zhu Rong** and the fifth generation of **Yandi,** **Gonggong** is the God of Water. Since he was not unhappy with **Zhuanxu,** he tried to usurp his throne as Central God of Heaven and fought with him, leading two subordinates **Xiangliu** and **Fuyou.** After his failure, he threw himself to Mount Buzhou.

Xingtian

Originally a subordinate of **Yandi,** he did not wish to be ruled by **Huangdi** and fought with him for his throne. After being defeated and beheaded, he still waved his shield and ax, using his nipples as eyes and navel as a mouth.

Goddess of Wushan

A daughter of **Yandi,** Yaoji was made **Wushan Goddess** by her father after her death.

Jingwei

The little daughter of **Yandi, Nuwa,** drowned in the sea and changed into a little bird named **Jingwei.**

Nüba

A daughter of **Huangdi** and a goddess, she once helped her father to defeat **Fengbo** and **Yushi,** who fought her father in support of **Chiyou.** She lost her power as a goddess during the war and could not return to the heaven. Wherever she stays, drought will occur.

Cangjie

A subordinate of **Huangdi,** he invented Chinese characters and later became his official historian.

Diku

The son of **Zhuanxu,** and great grandson of **Huangdi,** he became emperor himself after his father. He married five wives and produced brilliant sons, such as **Qi,** the forefather of the Shang clan, Houji, forefather of the Zhou clan and **Emperor Yao.**

Ebo

Being the eldest son of **Diku**, he was on bad terms with his younger brother **Shichen**. His father sent him to Shangqiu in the east. He stole kindling from heaven and brought it to earth.

Zigu

The daughter of **Diku**, she became a goddess after death and was able to predict whether it would be successful to raise silkworms in the following year.

Panhu

Being the ancestor of Yao and She people, **Panhu** was originally a dragon dog. He made contributions to the war in **Diku**'s time and married the daughter of **Diku**. The couple lived in deep mountain forests and their later generations formed the Yao and She nationalities.

Emperor Yao

The son of **Diku** and **Qingdu** and great-grandson of the **Yellow Emperor** was a sage of extraordinary virtue and also the greatest emperor of prehistoric times. During his rule, he encountered the calamity of ten suns appearing simultaneously in the sky, which caused a severe drought. He sent the archer **Yi** to shoot the suns. Followed the drought he encountered a deluge caused by **Gonggong**, God of Water, and sent **Gun** to control the flood. But **Gun** failed. **Emperor Yao** passed the throne to **Shun**, known for his high morals and brilliance.

Yi

Yi was good at archery. He received an order to teach the ten suns a lesson and shot down nine of them. He also fought the monsters that had brought destruction to human beings. But God abrogated his divine status. Since then, Yi had to live in the world of men. He went to Kunlun Mountain to see the **Western Mother Goddess** and obtained the pill of immortality. However, the pill was taken by his wife **Chang'e** and **Yi** was forced to stay in the world of men. He was later assassinated by his apprentice **Pangmeng** and ended his life tragically.

Gun

Grandson of the **Yellow Emperor**, he received **Emperor Yao**'s order to control the floods. He went to the heaven and stole a piece of the special soil, Xirang, to block the floodwater. God sent **Zhurong**, the God of Fire, to put him to death and took back the soil. The floods made a comeback and inundated lands once more. The God had people cut Gun's belly after his death; a dragon emerged from his belly and rose to the sky. This dragon was **Gun**'s son, **Dayu**.

Chang'e

Yi's wife **Chang'e** used to be an immortal in heaven and came to the world of men with **Yi**. Later she took the pill of immortality and flew to the moon alone to become the lonely Goddess of the Moon, accompanied by a white rabbit.

Emperor Shun

Legend has it that Emperor Shun was the eighth generation of **Yellow Emperor**'s offspring, a model of noble-minded behavior. His father, step mother and younger brother treated him cruelly and attempted to kill him many times. However, he treated them kindly as if nothing had happened. Forced to flee away from home, he was later selected as the successor of the throne and married **Emperor Yao**'s two daughters **Ehuang** and **Nüying**. He then reunited with the family, and his parents and younger brother were touched. After a series of tests, he finally succeeded to the throne from **Emperor Yao**. He sent **Dayu** to control the floods and finally achieved success. In his later years, **Emperor Shun** passed his power to Dayu and went to a tour of the country, but unfortunately he died of illness on his way.

Dayu

Son of **Gun**, a hero who tamed the floods. He led the deities to expel **Gonggong** and killed his underling **Xiangliu**. He dug channels to conduct water to the sea and controlled the Yellow River, Huai River and other rivers. He was hard-working and never went into his home although he passed it nine times. He turned into a bear to chisel the mountain faster and was found by his wife **Nüjiao**. Nüjiao ran away and turned into a huge stone before **Dayu** was able to catch up. The huge stone split and a boy emerged from it. He was Qi, the creator of the first Chinese dynasty—Xia. Dayu succeeded the throne from **Emperor Shun** after he controlled the floods.

Kuafu

The eighth generation offspring of **Emperor Yan** and grandson of **Houtu**, God of Earth, was a giant and excellent at running. He chased after the Sun to compete with it. Because he went too close to the Sun, he felt extremely thirsty and finally died in the wildness in the Northwest. His walking stick turned into a huge, lush peach forest. His offspring founded the country named Kuafu.

Appendix 2
Chronological Table of the Chinese Dynasties

The Paleolithic Period	c.1,700,000–10,000 years ago
The Neolithic Period	c. 10,000–4,000 years ago
Xia Dynasty	2070–1600 BC
Shang Dynasty	1600–1046 BC
Western Zhou Dynasty	1046–771 BC
Spring and Autumn Period	770–476 BC
Warring States Period	475–221 BC
Qin Dynasty	221–206 BC
Western Han Dynasty	206 BC–AD 25
Eastern Han Dynasty	25–220
Three Kingdoms	220–280
Western Jin Dynasty	265–317
Eastern Jin Dynasty	317–420
Northern and Southern Dynasties	420–589
Sui Dynasty	581–618
Tang Dynasty	618–907
Five Dynasties	907–960
Northern Song Dynasty	960–1127
Southern Song Dynasty	1127–1276
Yuan Dynasty	1276–1368
Ming Dynasty	1368–1644
Qing Dynasty	1644–1911
Republic of China	1912–1949
People's Republic of China	Founded in 1949